IMAGES
of England

PADDINGTON

St Augustine's church from Kilburn Park Road, *c.* 1912. This grand church with its steeple and spire towers 254ft above the streets of northern Paddington. The church by noted architect of fine churches, J.L. Pearson, was built 1870-1877 but the great Normandy-Gothic steeple was only completed in 1898, from which time it made a dramatic sight when seen from the surrounding Victorian streets. Tower blocks built nearby in postwar years have somewhat lessened the effect. The view reveals a row of long-vanished shops in Kilburn Park Road with Rudolph Road crossing beyond them and the lamp of the former Pembroke pub on the left.

IMAGES
of England

PADDINGTON

Brian Girling

TEMPUS

Bayswater Fire Station, Queen's Road (Queensway), *c*. 1904. Bayswater Fire Station opened in 1904 and closed in 1935 but the handsome building can still be seen in its new role as Claremont Court, a block of flats. On either side of the fire station are parts of the terraces which formerly made up Pickering Place which arose in the 1820s as one of the earliest urban developments hereabouts. The road was subsequently added to Queen's Road and renamed Queensway in 1939. The Queen's cinema was built to the right in 1936.

First published 2001, reprinted 2005

Tempus Publishing Limited
The Mill, Brimscombe Port,
Stroud, Gloucestershire, GL5 2QG
www.tempus-publishing.com

British Library Cataloguing in Publication Data.
A catalogue record for this book is available from the British Library.

ISBN 0 7524 2204 9

Typesetting and origination by Tempus Publishing Limited.
Printed in Great Britain.

Contents

A Paddington corner: Warren's Saddlery, Westbourne Park Road by Richmond Road (Chepstow Road), *c.* 1904. Although mechanically propelled vehicles were appearing in increasing numbers, early Edwardian London was still a city which relied on the horse for street transportation, ensuring lively business for emporia like Henry Warren's saddlery which had been established in 1860. Some of Paddington's vast equine population was well served here with a fine selection of harnesses, saddles, collars and nosebags. This image with Harry Warren and his assistant preserves a scene which would have been commonplace a century ago. The heavy coal wagon, left, belonged to a neighbouring business, that of Walter Moore, coal merchant of No. 69b Richmond Road – he was doubtless a client of the Warren saddlery. Richmond Road was renamed Chepstow Road in 1939.

Introduction

This book completes the trilogy of volumes which take a nostalgic look at the three boroughs that in 1965 were merged to create the modern City of Westminster. The third of these, the Metropolitan Borough of Paddington, is now a richly diverse slice of inner West London, but a mere two hundred years ago there was little more than a trio of scattered villages deep in the Middlesex countryside.

The evidence of Man's earliest activities in the area that would become Paddington is still with us, the long straight roads laid down in the first millenium by the Romans and which still follow much of their original routes – we know them now as Bayswater and Edgware Roads. By 1800, the village of Paddington comprised a scattering of houses and a manor surrounding a tiny church, with Westbourne Green and Bayswater just isolated hamlets.

A vast change was at hand, however, with the arrival in 1801 of the Grand Junction Canal followed by the development of the railways and a great terminus for London in Paddington. At the same time, London was expanding rapidly across its countryside, and the dawning of the nineteenth century heralded Paddington's transition from rural isolation to a busy city suburb. The photographs that follow are mostly from Edwardian days when Paddington station was a mighty monument to the age of steam and the streets were full of horse-drawn traffic. However the first generation of motors was making an appearance and there was electric public transport running above and below ground. There is a long look at the cool elegant terraces which made up the new Bayswater, and at the historic Royal Parks with their magnificent lake, an animal's graveyard and a statue to one of the most beloved characters in children's fiction. The photographs show the rise of one of the more famous London department stores and take a look at a street where all is not what it seems!

Chapter Two begins at a Roman crossroads which would later earn notoriety as a place of public execution, and goes on to explore ancient Watling Street, the Edgware Road, as it runs northwestwards to Maida Vale. There is a look at a royal Diamond Jubilee, the music hall where Marie Lloyd wowed her adoring audiences and at 'Venice in London' where Paddington's waterways have created a landscape unique in London. A photographic journey along historic Harrow Road revives memories of the little that remained of old Paddington before the destructive motorway building from the 1960s, and takes a look at the faintly Gothic houses at Queens Park where the shortest street name in London could once have been found. A look at Paddington's transport reveals the first underground railway in the world, a unique horse bus and the tracks upon which a tram only ran once a year. The book concludes with a tour of northern Paddington where gracious mansion flats were built on the last of the area's greenfield sites, the story of the world's biggest roller skating rink and a splendid children's party.

Most of the photographs have been gathered from private sources and have never appeared in print before.

Brian Girling
February 2001

Westbourne Grove by Hereford Road, *c*. 1920. Westbourne Grove began life as a rural lane in the countryside to the west of London, but following the opening of the Great Western Railway's London terminus, Paddington station, the lane began to take on a more residential aspect. It would take nearly twenty years for the first shop to arrive in what was to become one of London's more notable retailing areas. The year 1863 proved to be rather momentous for Westbourne Grove with the opening of the original section of the world's first underground railway from the City of London to Bishops Road, Paddington, together with the arrival of Paddington's most famous retailer, William Whiteley, the 'Universal Provider' who opened the first of his shops that year. Within another decade, Westbourne Grove was lined with fashionable department stores whose appeal was second only to those of the West End. The view catches Westbourne Grove early in the 1920s when the road was still fashionable and the weary shopper could relax for a while in the Grove Palace Cinema whose tiny frontage can be seen in the centre of the picture, just beyond Hereford Road. The cinema opened around 1920 but by 1931 it was known as the Roxy, and rather grandly in its final years before closure in the mid-1960s, the International Film Theatre.

One

Bayswater

Bayswater is the southern part of Paddington, the area north and west of the Roman roads we now know as Bayswater and Edgware Roads. Bayswater Road (Uxbridge Road until 1880) was once part of the Roman Via Trinobantia, the highway which ran in a mostly straight line from the City of London in a westerly direction, passing as it did so a spring where horses were watered. This became known in medieval times as Bayard's Watering, hence the names Bayswater. Apart from a scattering of cottages and inns, the Bayswater/Uxbridge Road remained in a rural state until around 1807 when the continuing expansion of London brought the tide of new housing to Tyburn (Marble Arch) and across the Edgware Road into what would, in time, form part of the Metropolitan Borough of Paddington. Tyburn was the site of what had been for many centuries London's busiest place of public execution, yet despite the notoriety of the name, a whole new quarter of London began to take shape bearing the name Tyburnia. Some of the first houses in Tyburnia were those seen in the photograph, part of Connaught Place which was built in 1807. The Tyburn names here actually come from a now subterranean stream - the Tyburn, and the gallows which were used from the twelfth to the eighteenth centuries were known as Tyburn Tree. The site of the gallows is behind the camera at Marble Arch, while in the distant part of the picture is Hyde Park Place with Tyburn Convent and the memorial to 105 martyrs who laid down their lives in defense of the Catholic faith from 1535-1681. These were the 'Tyburn Martyrs' who died on Tyburn's gallows during the Reformation.

Hyde Park Terrace (now Hyde Park Place) by Albion Street, Bayswater Road, *c.* 1904. As the urbanization of Tyburn/Bayswater proceeded, fine terraces of elegant stucco-fronted houses began to line Bayswater Road and the new streets leading off it. These examples date from the 1830s, but a century later modern apartment blocks began to replace the terraces and capitalise on the unrivalled views over Hyde Park. The twin blocks of Albion Gate replaced most of what is seen here in 1935.

Hyde Park Square, *c.* 1905. By early Victorian times the architecture of the terraces then being built had evolved into the grander Italianate style which was to become the norm for much of Bayswater. However from the 1930s, redevelopment and war damage was to cost Bayswater some of its distinctive townscape such as that seen here.

Victoria Gate and Victoria Lodge, Hyde Park, c. 1925. The history of Hyde Park dates back to 1536 when its area, part of the Manor of Hyde, was acquired and enclosed by Henry VIII to create a deer park for hunting. Eventually the public was allowed in, and it became a favourite resort of Londoners, one of the string of Royal Parks which ran from Bayswater almost to the Thames at Westminster. The view looks across Bayswater Road, with its No. 12 bus, to the terraces of Hyde Park Gardens and Stanhope Street and beyond to the magnificence that was once Sussex Square.

The Pet's Cemetery, Victoria Lodge, Bayswater Road, c. 1915. Around 300 pets were interred in this corner of the park from 1880-1967 when no further burials were allowed. One of the first interments in 1880 was that of the Duchess of Cambridge's favourite dog which had been run over in Bayswater Road. This gave the cemetery something of a social cachet and for a while it was the smart place in which to lay the dear departed to rest. Cats and other animals have also been buried in this peaceful place each with its tiny but sometimes ornate tombstone. One notable example marks the grave of a much-loved guide dog and has an inscription in braille.

The Long Water (the Serpentine) and the Peter Pan statue, Kensington Gardens, 1920. The Serpentine, the Paddington end of which is known as the Long Water, is the most visible evidence of the Westbourne stream, a now subterranean brook whose waters were used to create this magnificent lake. The Serpentine dates from 1730 when, by command of Queen Caroline, wife of George II, the Westbourne was dammed at a spot now known as the Dell allowing the waters to fill the natural valley of the stream along its course through Kensington Gardens and Hyde Park. The original river is unseen now, one of the lost rivers of London, its water being culverted along its course from Hampstead to the Thames. It is to here in an idyllic spot on a slight hill overlooking the lake that generations of children have come to visit the statue of one of the most beloved of characters in children's fiction, 'Peter Pan'. Local author J.M. Barrie's immortal 'boy who wouldn't grow up' was introduced in 1898 in a book called *The Little White Bird* and as a stage play *Peter Pan* which opened at the Duke of York's Theatre at Christmas 1904. In 1906 the Peter Pan story appeared in a new book *Peter Pan in Kensington Gardens*. A statue of Peter Pan in bronze was created by Sir George Frampton, and at the insistence of J.M. Barrie, and to add to the magic, it was put up in the dead of night on 30 April 1912. The story was that it had been carried to the park by the fairies. Naturally, children were entranced by this and have been drawn to Peter's statue ever since, their hands having given a fine polish to the small bronze animals and fairies which encircle the statue's pedestal.

A further consequence of the Peter Pan story was the emergence of the Christian name 'Wendy'. A century ago there was no one anywhere called Wendy, the name being introduced by Barrie in the story and due to the nature of this character the name's future popularity was assured. A new childrens playground in Kensington Gardens has been built in memory of Princess Diana, featuring elements of the Peter Pan tale including a splendid pirate ship to play on. This spring time photograph shows everyone enjoying a stroll in the park, a timeless scene apart from the 1920s fashions seen here. The beautiful Italian Water Gardens, laid out in 1861, are visible in the distance.

Sussex Square, *c.* 1904. Sussex Square was begun in 1843 and was named after Prince Augustus, Duke of Sussex, the sixth son of George III. The houses typified the grand designs of Tyburnia and Bayswater – one of those shown would attract Winston Churchill who came to live at No. 2 from 1920-1924 while he was Secretary for War and Colonial Secretary. Admiral Jellicoe took No. 26 after the Battle of Jutland. The splendour of these houses has not saved them and from 1933 smaller, plainer houses began to replace them.

Sussex Square, *c.* 1904. Grand Corinithian columns and an ornate frieze characterized these early Victorian town houses on the western side of Sussex Square. In common with the rest of the square, the houses have been replaced but in Bathurst Street, right, some old buildings still stand.

Stanhope Street, *c.* 1906. Another piece of Bayswater's vanished townscape with smart modern houses taking the place of their Victorian predecessors, seen here in Edwardian days.

Gloucester Square, *c.* 1906. More variations on the theme of the large Victorian town house, these ones sporting unusually spacious porches and wide basement areas. These too have vanished in favour of three-storey terraces built in the 1930s.

14

Stanhope Terrace, Bayswater Road, *c.* 1903. Old houses and the Crown pub which stood on the site of the towering Royal Lancaster Hotel. Visible here is the single storey Lancaster Gate station on the then newly opened Central London Railway (Central Line, see p. 104).

Stanhope Terrace, Bayswater Road, *c.* 1937. A comparison view showing how this part of Bayswater Road had changed over some thirty-four years. By this time, Lancaster Gate station had been topped by the Park Gate Hotel, while further along by Lancaster Terrace there is modernity amidst the Victoriana with the Fountains apartments which had replaced the older properties earlier in the 1930s. A noticeable dip in the road clearly reveals the old valley of the Westbourne stream. Much of the nearer property was replaced in 1968 with the Royal Lancaster Hotel, a scheme which entailed road widening and a new Lancaster Gate station.

Lancaster Street from Lancaster Gate, *c.* 1905. Lancaster Street, a service street for the large town houses which surrounded it was renamed Barrie Street in 1939 in celebration of local author J.M. Barrie. Barrie Street's existence was all too brief, however, for during October 1940 the street was destroyed by a land mine and subsequently built over, the name living on as the Barrie Estate; Carroll House now stands on the line of the old street. A group of youths is standing by Elms Mews, a byway which existed as Elms Lane in Bayswater rural past.

Lancaster Street, *c.* 1920. A later view of old Lancaster Street with St James church, Sussex Gardens (now the parish church of Paddington) seen from what is now an impossible viewpoint with the disappearance of the street. Lancaster Street comprised of a number of domestic stores, a garage, post office, the Devonshire Arms pub and a number of hotels.

Marlborough Gate, Bayswater Road, *c.* 1904. Grand Victorian houses crowd in upon the tiny Swan centre, an inn established around 1775 on the Uxbridge (Bayswater) Turnpike Road. Here too were the Floral Tea Gardens with a skittle alley and other rural attractions, the picturesque nature of the place surviving to this day, with a leafy forecourt overlooking the park.

Lancaster Gate, *c.* 1906. The *grandeur* of the terraces facing the park rose to new heights with the building in 1856-1857 of Lancaster Gate with its colonnaded balconies, but the insertion of a postwar red brick apartment block in the middle of the row has since disrupted the symmetry of the design.

Leinster Corner (now No. 100 Bayswater Road), by Leinster Terrace, c. 1906. Leinster Corner was the home of J.M. Barrie and his family from 1902-1909 and a most agreeable one for the author who could just step across Bayswater Road to stroll in his beloved Kensington Gardens. Barrie was living at Leinster Corner when this picture was taken, the year in which *Peter Pan in Kensington Gardens* was published. The photograph is a postcard sent by a neighbour who writes 'this card is a view of Mr Barrie's house'.

Leinster Terrace, c. 1906. This charming terrace of Victorian shops was a stone's throw from Leinster Corner, doubtless a useful amenity for the Barrie family. It was entirely possible that the author may have purchased his stationery from the shop of Crockett & Co., newsagents and stationers, whose premises are seen on the left.

Leinster Gardens, London, W. No. 8057.

Leinster Gardens, *c.* 1926. At first glance this may look like a typical Bayswater Street with its long Italianate terrace but a closer look at the houses centre left (with the lighter paint work) will reveal some of Bayswater's more notable curiosities, for two of the buildings are not houses at all, just false fronts. The story began in the early 1850s when Leinster Gardens was built but after just a decade of uneventful existence, the lives of the residents were thrown into turmoil when the Metropolitan Railway Company announced its plans for extending their line in a cutting from Paddington to Brompton (Gloucester Road) – right through the new terrace. Naturally the householders objected to having their lovely new street despoiled in this way but a compromise was at hand and although two of the houses had to be demolished, their façades were retained, bridging the cutting when the railway was built and opened in 1868. The dummy houses had a further advantage by preventing some of the vapours from the old Metropolitan steam locomotives from escaping into the street. This ceased to be a problem following the early twentieth century electrification of the line. The trains of the District and Circle Lines still rattle through the cutting, most of their passengers unaware of this unique feature of the Underground high above them. The 'houses' can still be seen at Nos 23 and 24 Leinster Gardens, their original features intact unlike many of the neighbouring properties which have been rebuilt or modernized.

Christ Church, Lancaster Gate, *c.* 1920. Christ Church was a suitably imposing building in the Gothic revival style set in the classical townscape of Bayswater, the church's tall spire making a notable landmark especially when seen from Kensington Gardens. It was built from 1854-1855 by F. & H. Francis but much of the church was replaced in 1983 by Spire House, a new residential block which mercifully retained the old tower and spire. The base of the tower is used as an entrance lobby with lifts to the upper floors.

Porchester Gate, Bayswater Road by Queensborough Terrace, *c.* 1906. This was another of the individually numbered terraces which made up Bayswater Road and a particularly impressive one with its double row of colonnaded balconies. Nothing remains of it, however, the modern flats of the new Porchester Gate taking its place.

Porchester Terrace, *c.* 1904. An earlier (1820s) street of stucco-fronted villas to contrast with the later terraces more usual in Bayswater. The spacious houses with their surrounding greenery have attracted several famous residents including Bayswater's retailing tycoon, William Whiteley and novelist Wilkie Collins who lived here with his father when still a child.

The new motor car, Porchester Terrace, 1904. Surgeon Robert Collie, his family and chauffeur prepare for a drive in their new car at Christmas time, 1904. The Collies lived at No. 25 Porchester Terrace in some affluence – private motoring was expensive in 1904 and could only be afforded by the well-to-do. The car's pristine condition would not have lasted long given the muddy state of the road.

Queen's Road (now Queensway) Underground station, Bayswater Road, c. 1904. Most of Victorian Coburg Terrace gave its site for Queen's Road station, a stop on what was then one of London's latest electronic wonders, the Central London Railway which conveyed its first passengers deep beneath Bayswater's streets on 30 July 1900. The street transport, however, was still that of the preceding century with the old Bayswater horse-bus route following that of the new Tube line on its journey from Shepherds Bush to the Bank of England. The bus had a good load of passengers even though the Tube would have made the journey in a fraction of the time. Beyond Queen's Road is Bayswater Hill and the Black Lion Pub – Black Lion Lane was an earlier name of Queen's Road. The pub was rebuilt in the nineteenth century.

Orme Court and Bark Place from Bayswater Road, c. 1905. Orme Court, right, with its rich terracotta embellishments dates from 1896 but the earlier houses in the background have given way to modern town houses.

Queen's Road (Queensway), *c.* 1905. Queensway, one of Bayswater's principal shopping streets began life as a rural byway called Westbourne Green Lane (it led to the village of Westbourne Green) before the first of its many renamings as Black Lion Lane after a local inn. Following the accession of Queen Victoria in 1837 the lane, which by now was beginning to be built up, was restyled Queen's Road in honour of the monarch who had spent much of her childhood at nearby Kensington Palace. In the 1930s, the London County Council embarked upon a programme of street renamings – there being an over abundance of Queen's Roads in London and Queensway was considered an attractive alternative for the Bayswater one. By this time, Queensway was well into its retailing heyday, the northern end of the street being dominated by the mighty emporium of William Whiteley. The picture looks back to Edwardian days in Queen's Road with Whiteley's away in the distance with a pair of flags flying from the roof and a host of smaller shops lining the road to compliment the great department store. The small shops on the left made way in the 1930s for the flats of Princes Court while beyond, a row of stone urns marks the position of Bayswater Underground Station whose opening on 1 October 1868 did much to stimulate Queen's Road's status as a shopping street. Almost hidden by the creeper, the Methodist Free Church (1868) can be seen on the right before its reincarnation in the 1950s as the Catholic Church of Our Lady, Queen of Heaven. In a city of cosmopolitan neighbourhoods, the Queensway of modern times is at the heart of one of London's more colourful and interesting districts with an exotic mix of Greek, Arabic and Chinese businesses, all overlooked by Whiteley's which has been reborn as a spectacular indoor shopping centre.

Queen's Road (Queensway) from Bayswater Road, c. 1920. It is 1920 and Queen's Road station, which would later change its name to Queensway along with the street, is seen again, but by comparison with the view on p. 22, it had been topped by the Coburg Court Hotel. Further along, the jumble of lowly properties were lingering remnants from the days when Queen's Road was called Black Lion Lane and a piecemeal development of small houses with generous front gardens was put up. This was rather grandly called Upper Craven Place and dated from the early nineteenth century when gaps between the scattered houses and villas of western Bayswater began to be filled in. As Queen's Road evolved into a shopping street, the long gardens were sacrificed in order that more shops could be built, a process typical of many a suburban main road in Victorian London. This untidy row of properties lingered on until 1928 when following demolition, the smart residential blocks of Queen's Court arose in their stead together with what is now London's oldest surviving ice skating rink, Queen's. The row of shops to the right of the picture concealed a most untypical Bayswater enterprise, Usher's Wiltshire Brewery. Everything on this site was replaced in 1968 by the ten-storied Consort House. The domed Whiteley building can be seen in the far distance, this being the first part of the great rebuilding of the store dating from 1911, while adjacent to the Tube station, left, is another Whiteley innovation, the column-mounted clock which was well placed to direct passengers emerging from the station towards the store. The Whiteley clock still stands, albeit in a modernized form.

Orme Square and Orme Court from Bayswater Road, *c*. 1905. Orme Square is the oldest of the Bayswater Squares and one of the smallest in London. It was built by Bond Street print seller Edward Orme around 1818 on land he owned beside Kensington Gravel Pits. While on a visit to London, the Czar of Russia, Alexander I is reputed to have purchased a consignment of local gravel for building construction in St Petersburgh – hence the Russian street names in this part of Bayswater. Orme Square's notable former residents included Sir Rowland Hill who in 1840 introduced the penny rate for letter post. Lord Leighton the painter also lived here.

St Petersburgh Place from Bayswater Road, *c*. 1903. The places of worship for three faiths can be found in close proximity here. To the left can be seen the slender tower and spire of St Matthew's (Anglican), built from 1881 on the site of the Bayswater Chapel. Opposite is the New West End synagogue, an opulent construction from the late 1870s with a much admired rose window, and in the distance but just out of sight is St Sophia's with its Byzantine domes. It was built in 1877 for wealthy Greek merchants living in Bayswater – it became the Greek Orthodox Cathedral in 1932.

George Taviner & Sons, Court Florist, Coburg Place, Bayswater Road, *c.* 1910. These premises were adjacent to Queen's Road (Queensway) Tube Station in Coburg Place, one of the smaller terraces which formerly made up Bayswater Road. The shop with its trio of charming lady assistants made an attractive sight, as did the neighbouring house with its greenery and stained glass door panels.

The Kings Head, Moscow Road, by Caroline Place, *c.* 1910. A typical corner pub with its moulded plasterwork and etched glass windows. It stands on the Moscow Road corner of Caroline Place, now Poplar Place and although rebuilt, it still retains its column-mounted pub sign. Moscow Road's name is another commemoration of the visit of the Czar of Russia around 1814.

Clifton Place from Sussex Place, c. 1909. A further example of the vanished townscape of Bayswater's hinterland with Clifton Place's bow-fronted houses leading into Sussex Square (see p. 13). Smart apartment blocks have replaced much of what is seen here.

Westbourne Street from Sussex Gardens, c. 1905. These houses from the 1830s were given bow fronts in order that their residents may have a better view of the park in the manner of the Regency houses of Brighton and elsewhere, where a view of the sea (and in Bayswater the park) was a good selling point. The only house not to have survived is at the far right, the site of the Royal Lancaster Hotel. Signs on the street lamps point the way to an assortment of railway stations.

Southwick Crescent (Hyde Park Crescent), *c.* 1906. The crescent is seen here with its original houses which vanished late in the 1930s and were replaced by the low-rise houses more familiar today. The houses face the church of St John the Evangelist with St Michael and All Angels, the latter part of the name referring to the former St Michael's near Edgware Road, whose congregation moved here following the closure of their own church.

Norfolk Crescent, *c.* 1905. Norfolk Crescent, part of the Hyde Park Estate, was to be comprehensively rebuilt in the 1960s when towering high-rise apartment blocks replaced these original houses. Norfolk Crescent still curves elegantly but the houses are strictly mid-twentieth century in style.

Devonport Street (Sussex Place) from Clifton Place, *c.* 1905. This street has retained many of its original houses in a handsome thoroughfare which leads onward to London Street and Paddington Station. The crossroads with Grand Junction Road (now Sussex Gardens) are seen on the right.

Grand Junction Road (Sussex Gardens) and Oxford Terrace, *c.* 1905. This broad avenue was once part of London's first bypass, the 'New Road' built in 1756 around what then was the city's rural perimeter. It later took the name Grand Junction Road after the local canal and waterworks which featured open reservoirs between London Street and Praed Street. The waterworks were incorporated in 1811 but moved to Kew in 1855. The Oxford and Cambridge Terraces were built on either side of Grand Junction Road in the 1840s but the part of Oxford Terrace seen here has been replaced by luxurious modern apartments.

Cambridge Terrace, Grand Junction Road (Sussex Gardens), *c.* 1925. The confusion of street names hereabouts was abolished in the 1930s when everything became Sussex Gardens, a pre-existing name for the terraces at the western end of Grand Junction Road. Hotels have long flourished here due to the proximity of Paddington Station.

All Saints, Norfolk Square, *c.* 1905. Norfolk Square was laid out in the mid-1850s and with it came the first All Saints, its burnt out ruins being replaced in 1895 by the building seen here with its unusual timbered gable and terracotta portico. The Royal Association for the Deaf and Dumb adopted the church from 1925 to 1960 when demolition was followed by the building of Edna House, a complex of flats for the retired.

London Street from Cambridge Terrace (Sussex Gardens), *c.* 1904. The nature of Bayswater's streets change with increasing proximity to Paddington Station, the Grand Junction (now the Grand Union) canal, and the commercial activites of the two organizations which did so much to shape the development of Paddington. Hotels and guest houses abound here and the streets are usually busy with the comings and goings of the great railway terminus. The shopping terrace on the left backs onto Talbot Square which was built on the site of one of the Grand Junction Water Company's reservoirs.

London Street from Cambridge Terrace, 1925. Hotels, including the former Sutherland House, centre, extend towards Paddington station whose distinctive roof is visible in the distance with the trees of Norfolk Square seen along the way. London Street was named after the landowners, the Bishops of London.

Spring Street, *c.* 1904. The street name recalls the aquatic nature of the area with the Westbourne stream flowing close by and a number of local springs and conduits. Conduit Mews whose covered entrance is seen by the cart, left, is another example. The terrace shops date from the 1840s – one of them is having its upper parts painted by a gentleman with a precarious perch on a ladder of dizzying height. There is a tempting offer of a dozen bottles of Medoc for 14s at the shop of George Baker, wine merchant on the left.

Spring Street, *c.* 1904. These two-storied basement houses have survived despite the commercial activities which, even in 1904 had infiltrated them. The further one was Harry Boyce's newsagent's shop with John Tayler, builder, next door. The larger block beyond has been replaced by the flats of Sussex Court.

Westbourne Terrace by Craven Road, *c.* 1920. This is another of Bayswater's grand boulevards stretching from Sussex Gardens almost to the railway where such *grandeur* comes to an abrupt halt. The houses were built from 1839 to the late 1850s, with the garden strips blocking out some of the traffic noise. The trees have matured into avenues of towering London Planes.

Gloucester Terrace, *c.* 1904. In a city of remarkable streets, Gloucester Terrace is surely one of the more noteworthy ones with its long panorama of bow-fronted terraces undulating towards a distant horizon, each curving window striving for a view of the park which grows ever more elusive the further north one goes.

Craven Terrace from Lancaster Mews, *c*. 1905. Despite some uncoordinated paintwork, this impressive local shopping terrace entered the twentieth century with all its architectural features intact including the intricate ironwork which runs the length of the row. The Mitre Hotel, left, exhibits the typical marbled stonework of the Victorian pub while a contrast is provided in the distance with the stone fronted St James's National School.

Craven Terrace from Craven Road, *c*. 1928. A view from the opposite end of Craven Terrace shows St James's National Schools once more, centre, while a vanished landmark can be seen opposite, Jehovah's Witnesses' London Tabernacle, a building which began life in 1862 as Craven Hill Congregational church. The site of the church has been filled by the Lancaster Hall Hotel.

Craven Road by Devonshire Terrace, *c.* 1905. Baker Walter Chilton shared his corner shop with Craven Road post office whose unusual square posting box is seen outside. The baker's boy is seen by the kerb, his cart loaded ready for the local deliveries. Further along was Stephen Matthews' butchers shop with a row of rabbits hanging up. The Matthews' delivery cart is also by the kerbside. One of the residential properties at the end of the row would later provide a home for Tommy Handley, the radio comedian who would keep the nation amused in the 1940s with his popular ITMA programme.

Craven Road by Eastbourne Terrace, *c.* 1905. Tradesmen in white aprons stand by their shops, one of which included Turner's bookshop and library. In an area like Bayswater where there were no public libraries emporia like Turner's provided a useful service – for a fee. The London Joint Stock Bank looks suitably stolid on its corner.

Cleveland Gardens, c. 1928. Cleveland Gardens typified the Victorian Bayswater garden square but this scene in postwar years looked very different with the building of the Hallfield Estate. The estate was designed in 1947 by the Tecton firm of architects for Paddington's postwar housing programme and featured six and ten-storey blocks of flats surrounded by a generous amount of greenery. The terrace on the right of the picture made way for part of the estate as did distant houses in Leinster Place where the ten-storey Reading House is now a dominating feature. The houses to the left and the garden are still in place.

The School of Woodcarving, No. 218 Gloucester Terrace, c. 1916. Miss Evelyn Chambers presided over this establishment in one of the Gloucester Terrace houses, where a group of mostly female pupils are seen learning the skills of woodcarving. Miss Chambers shared the house with her artist sister Diana.

LONDON. Bishop's Road, Paddington. No. 1788.

Bishop's Road (Bishop's Bridge Road) from Westbourne Terrace, *c.* 1923. This is another of Paddington's roads which is far older than its Victorian buildings would suggest, having originated as a leafy footpath linking the isolated settlements of Paddington and Westbourne Green, crossing the Westbourne stream at a bridge which would, from the 1930s, form part of its name. The 'Bishops' were the Bishops of London who were granted these Paddington lands by Edward VI in the sixteenth century. The nineteenth century gave Bishop's Road the urban appearance seen in the photograph, with the stuccoed terraces being offset by the soaring Gothic spire of Holy Trinity church, built from 1843-1846 by Thomas Cundy, the renowned architect of fine Victorian churches. The church has fallen victim to redevelopment and there are flats here now, as there are to the right where Brewer's Court has replaced the shopping parade. A lofty ladder rises from the pavement to attic level, centre.

Bishop's Road (Bishop's Bridge Road) with Westbourne Grove, c. 1905. This shows a view at the western end of Bishop's Road by Inverness Terrace with the shopping centre of Westbourne Grove in the distance. This area was mostly built up in the 1850s with shops being concentrated along the rather narrow Westbourne Grove from Chepstow Road in the west to Bishop's Road in the east. This was an outer suburb of London in the 1850s and was somewhat remote from the city before the underground railway arrived in the 1860s so it took an adventurous soul to set up business here. Many ventures failed and for a while Westbourne Grove was derided as 'Bankruptcy Row'. It was to this unlikely location that Yorkshireman William Whiteley, having been inspired by the wonders he had seen at the Great Exhibition in Hyde Park in 1851, and having learnt the drapery trade at a succession of London emporia, opened in 1862 a single shop selling ribbons and fancy goods. The shop prospered and Whiteley acquired further Westbourne Grove properties which he turned into an impressive department store, expanding further into Queen's Road. The opening of the railways further secured the status of the area, no longer 'Bankruptcy Row' but the 'Bond Street of the West', where fashionable Victorian ladies flocked to spend their guineas in the smart new shops. A further success story was that of Welshman William Owen who opened the Bayswater Trimming Shop in 1873 opposite Whiteley's and similarly expanded along Westbourne Grove and into Hatherley Grove. When Whiteley's concentrated their efforts in Queen's Road in 1911, Owen was left to rule the roost in Westbourne Grove, together with Bradley's department store, by Chepstow Road. Other prominent stores abounded including a branch of Hope Brothers, the outfitters, seen here on its Bishop's Road/Porchester corner where the modern Colonnades complex now stands. Further along is the still extant Royal Oak pub, an 1870 rebuilding of the original Royal Oak, a tavern and tea gardens which once stood surrounded by fields near the village of Westbourne Green. The pub provided a useful stopping place for horse buses until Edwardian times. The small shops by Queen's Road were replaced by the Queen's cinema in 1936.

38

Whiteley's store, Westbourne Grove, c. 1908. Part of the long run of what were once individual shops were acquired by William Whiteley as part of his expanding department store. The shop proudly displays its royal warrant 'by special appointment to H.M. the King' (Edward VII), an honour previously held during the reign of Victoria. The windows are seen crammed with merchandise, as was usual during Edwardian times.

Queen's Road (Queensway), c. 1906. Whiteley's original premises in Queen's Road are seen with their monster flagpole and banner proclaiming Whiteley's as the 'universal providers'. To the left were the Paddington Public Baths which were built by the former Paddington Vestry and opened in 1874. The sites would soon be cleared for the first part of the grand new Whiteley store, while in the background the grim and grimy Pickering Place preceded a more fashionable later life as part of Queensway. Inver Court, with its shops and flats would eventually replace residential Queen's Terrace, right.

Whiteley's, Queen's Road (Queensway), *c.* 1920. During the last years of the Edwardian era, it became apparent that Whiteley's was outgrowing its existing premises and a plan of rebuilding was put into operation. Designed by Belcher & Jones, the first part of the 'New Whiteley's' (as it was then called) was opened by the Lord Mayor of London on a bright, sunny 21 November 1911, with the Mayor and Mayoress of Paddington among a host of dignitaries in attendance and such a throng of onlookers that a considerable police presence was needed to control the crowds. The Paddington Baths site was used first – the Victorian part of the store can still be seen in the picture as it juts out further along. It would not be until 1925 that the great façade would be completed when it took in the last of the Victorian Whiteley's, completing a long run from Porchester Gardens to Redan Place. The great store prospered but eventually declined, closing in 1981. However the building lived on and reopened on 26 July 1989 as Whiteley's Shopping Centre, a vast and spectacular indoor shopping complex which retained the best of the original architecture. The old houses of the former Queen's Terrace are again seen here, and beyond them and just visible, part of one of Paddington's first cinemas, the tiny Queen's Road Cinematograph Theatre which opened around 1911. It was known at various times as the Eldorado and the PeepShow Cinema before closing around 1926. There are modern flats and shops here now, one of which, No. 184 Queensway, was the location of this country's first self service launderette which was opened on 9 May 1949 by the Bendix Company. The first ever Bendix was opened in New York in 1945. To the right of the picture, the gabled Paddington Charity School on the Porchester Gardens corner is framed by an ornate hanging lamp attached to the Prince Alfred Hotel.

Westbourne Grove form Queen's Road (Queensway), *c.* 1926. A busy scene in Westbourne Grove with a kerbside flower seller set up outside another large store, that of Henry Dobb, drapers. The Redan pub on the Queen's Road corner, left dates from 1855, its name commemorating a British attack on a fortress of that name during the Crimean War.

Westbourne Grove Terrace from Westbourne Grove, *c.* 1905. The shops of Whiteley's great rival, William Owen, occupy both corners of this side street which was almost entirely made up of lodging houses provided by Whiteley's for their female shop staff. For these ladies, the regime at Whiteley's was an oppressive one with the working day lasting from 7 a.m. to 11 p.m. and there was an obligation to vacate the lodging houses during their few days off. The houses on the right have been replaced by the 1930s flats of Hatherley Court and the United Presbyterian Church (1863), later St Paul's, has been demolished following closure in 1970.

Westbourne Grove by Westbourne Grove Terrace, c. 1910. Although William Owen did not have the grand purpose built emporium favoured by William Whiteley, the selling space in an assortment of buildings almost rivalled that of his competitor but the operation was not as durable as that of Whiteley, and Owen's had closed by 1929. To the left of the view is the Gothic frontage of Westbourne Hall which is in use here as Whiteley's estate agents department. The building, which in the 1860s and 1970s was used for a variety of theatrical entertainments, is seen here being brightened up with a coat of paint.

Hatherley Grove from Westbourne Grove, c. 1905. In common with William Whiteley, William Owen also provided residential accommodation for his employees – the houses can be seen on the right. To the left of the picture onlookers admire the chauffeur driven automobile which presumably belonged to one of Owen's wealthy clients.

Westbourne Grove, c. 1904. Shoppers crowd the street and a trio of oriental sandwich men proclaim the delights of the Pagoda Restaurant at No. 70 Westbourne Grove in which diners were serenaded by the Pagoda Orchestra. The lowlier buildings in the centre of the view are surviving remnants of the villas which lined Westbourne Grove before the shops began to arrive in 1854.

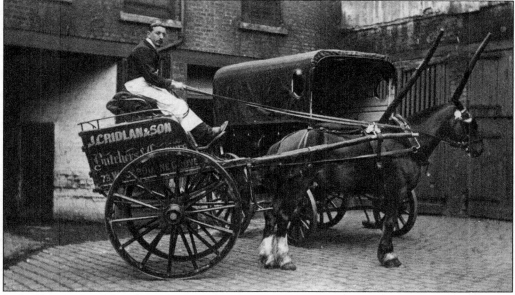

J. Cridlan & Sons, butchers, No. 73 Westbourne Grove, c. 1920. The shop in Westbourne Grove was part of a chain of such establishments run by the Cridlan family. One of the company's delivery carts is seen here in a local mews where it was stabled overnight.

Porchester Road, *c.* 1905. The Westbourne Grove/Queen's Road retailing area also took in the southern part of Porchester Road although the shops here tended to be rather more modest. An exception was linen draper Robert Davies' premises, which ran some distance along an old row of buildings once known as Pickering Terrace. These have been replaced by Peter's Court, an apartment block of 1930s vintage, while the further part of the site was used for Porchester Hall (1925-1929), Paddington's municipal assembly hall, baths and library.

Porchester Road looking towards Bishop's (Bridge) Road and Inverness Terrace, *c.* 1910. A view predating the building of Peter's Court on the right and the later Colonnades on the left. In this much-changed scene, the distant block by Inverness Terrace gave its site for part of the modern Hallfield Estate.

Hereford Road by Princes Square and Dawson Place, c. 1905. A busy moment in the history of Hereford Square with the coalman on his rounds, a delivery boy with his barrow and the wagon of Lowe & Sons, bakers taking on a load of loaves for local households. The Prince Edward pub, left, was named after Queen Victoria's eldest son, the future Edward VII and beyond it the serpentine facades of Hereford Road's bow fronted town houses undulate towards distant Westbourne Grove.

The Princess Royal, Hereford Road, c. 1907. The pub was opened in the 1840s by James Bott (whose name lives on in Bott's Mews at the rear of the premises), and soon became a popular rural resort with an archery ground and bowling green before new houses closed upon it in the 1850s.

Monmouth Road from Westbourne Grove, *c*. 1907. This street was laid out from the 1840s and 50s with two-storied stoccoed villas which enjoyed rural views before later terraces of town houses brought increasing urbanisation. The baker's boy form Arthur's Stores Bakery in Richmond (Chepstow) Road is seen attending to his wares while behind him another youth takes advantage of the peaceful Edwardian traffic conditions to work from a handcart in the middle of the road. To the left was a cookery school run by Miss Roberta Rees at No. 78 Westbourne Grove.

Ilchester Gardens by Moscow Road, *c*. 1907. Large Victorian town houses in a variety of styles, some featuring unpainted stucco fronts which tended to blacken in the sooty London air.

Norfolk Road (Needham Road), *c.* 1907. This short street appears little changed in nearly a century, its shops and bow-fronted houses facing each other across an unusually wide roadway. To the right, Wellington Mews West has since acquired the equally splendid name of Pentagram Yard.

St Mary of the Angels, Westmoreland Road (Moorhouse Road), *c.* 1910. The building of this busy Catholic church, which initially served a congregation of Irish immigrants, began in 1851 with the following decades seeing further additions to the structure. The tower was completed in the twentieth century replacing the ugly wooden affair seen in the photograph. Priests of the Order of St Charles Borromeo ministered here for over a century and the church retains a cosmopolitan congregation for whom a weekly Portuguese Mass is provided. The handsome Parish House is seen on the left with luxuriant creeper partly obscuring the brickwork and the bands of stone which match those of the church.

Richmond Road (Chepstow Road), *c.* 1910. This corner is still recognisable with its small shops on either side of the tiny but decidedly quaint Bott's Mews but the taller building which housed the china and glass departments of another of Westbourne Grove's major stores, Arthur's, has gone. Bott's Mews, centre, had an elegant balustraded archway entrance but its walls had disappeared under a mass of fly-posting. The further side turning, Victoria Place, was renamed Bridstow Place in the 1930s.

Talbot Road by Shrewsbury Road, *c.* 1910. The houses were overlooked by a tall spire which belonged to St Stephen's church, Westbourne Park Road. The church was built from 1855 but in 1950 the spire was found to be unsafe and demolished. Talbot Road is crossed by Richmond Road (Chepstow Road), centre, where the Artesian pub may be seen. The pub was later renamed after Louis Lucien Bonaparte, nephew of Napoleon III, a one-time resident of Westbourne Grove.

Two
Edgware Road, Maida Vale and Little Venice

LONDON. Edgware Road. No. 1287.

Edgware Road and its northern continuation, Maida Vale separate the former boroughs of Marylebone and Paddington, the straightness of the road a legacy of its Roman origins as Watling Street. The Romans constructed the local section of their great highway on the slightly elevated ground between the two streams which would later be called the Westbourne and the Tyburn, crossing another Roman Road, the Via Trinobantia, the future Oxford Street and Bayswater Road. Apart from a number of historic inns which had grown to cater for travellers on Watling Street, the road to Edgware remained in a largely rural state until the beginning of the nineteenth century but London was expanding rapidly across its countryside, eventually catching up with Edgware Road, first on the Marylebone side and subsequently as the new suburb of Tyburnia on the Paddington side. The tide of building spread along the Edgware Road and surrounded the village of Paddington with new developments, a process given impetus by the opening of the Grand Junction Canal in 1801. Edgware Road went on to acquire many of the characteristics typical of main roads in London's nineteenth century suburbs with rows of small shops topped by living space with a pub always close at hand and carriageways filled with clamouring traffic. London continued to grow and Edgware Road became 'inner city' rather than suburban, and during the twentieth century some of the humble shopping parades began to be replaced by smart new apartment blocks.

Marble Arch, Oxford Street and Edgware Road, c. 1925. The old Tyburn area took the name of Marble Arch after the structure which was moved here in 1851, having originally been created in 1828 as an entrance to Buckingham Palace. Edgware Road is seen striking off at an angle to the left, with the houses of Connaught Place close by. In the centre of the picture is a row of grand town houses which would soon be replaced by the luxurious Regal (later Odeon) cinema and in turn in 1963 by a new Odeon and a monstrously overbearing tower block.

Marble Arch and 'Tyburn Gallows', *c.* 1927. A photograph of poor quality but one which unusually shows a reproduction of the Tyburn gallows in the position where they stood from the fourteenth to the eighteenth centuries. Prior to the construction of the triangular gallows, the local trees served a similar purpose, hence the term 'Tyburn Tree' which persisted for many centuries. The hangings at Tyburn were a considerable public spectacle to the point where viewing galleries were put up to accommodate the crowds. From 1783 the executions took place at Newgate Prison but there is a plaque in the roadway to mark the spot where the Tyburn gallows once stood.

Edgware Road from Connaught Place, *c.* 1910. Plain brick terraces of shops characterised Victorian Edgware Road but by Edwardian days, newer, grander buildings were taking their place. One of these was the store of C. Cozens, linen drapers, who built their premises in 1909 on the Seymour Street corner. To the left, part of the long vanished Mitre pub is seen on the opposite Seymour Street.

Connaught Street from Cambridge Street (Kendal Street), *c.* 1906. Modest terraced houses dating from the 1820s in one of the earlier streets built off the Edgware Road. Three of the shops seen here then accommodated a branch of Society caterers Searcy, Tansley & Co. who were founded in 1847.

Connaught Square by Portsea Place, *c.* 1906. Dating from 1821, this was the first square to be built in Tyburnia, the site being close to a ramshackle temporary settlement known as Tomlin's New Town which had sprung up in the fields around 1790. The square remains wonderfully unspoilt and has a charm sometimes missing from the grander squares of Bayswater. A 'blue plaque' commemorates ballerina Marie Taglioni who lived at No. 14 from 1875 to 1876.

Waiting for the Queen, Victoria's Diamond Jubilee, Edgware Road by Cambridge Street (Kendal Street), 21 June 1897. Edgware Road is not famed as a royal processional route but due to its position between Buckingham Palace and Paddington station where royal trains from Windsor terminate, it has sometimes been used as one. Such an occasion occurred during the hot, sunny June of 1897 as the nation celebrated the Diamond Jubilee of Queen Victoria. Jubilee Day was the 22 June and on the previous day, Her Majesty took the royal train from Windsor, duly arriving at a lavishly decorated Paddington station where she received London's first Jubilee greeting from Paddington as represented by the administrative Vestry. Queen Victoria was also presented with an illuminated address which referred to the growth of Paddington's population from 20,000 to 125,000 during the 60 years of the Queen's reign. The Royal party then proceeded in a carriage procession to Buckingham Palace to prepare for the celebrations of Jubilee day itself, the route including Grand Junction Road (Sussex Gardens) where Paddington's picturesque commemorative archway had been erected and Edgware Road where another archway (seen on the left of the photograph) had been put up by the Vestry of St Marylebone. On Jubilee Day there was a grand parade through the streets of London to the steps of St Paul's Cathedral where a service of thanksgiving was held, the Queen remaining in her carriage due to her physical frailty. The Jubilee was celebrated with great fervour in Paddington where many buildings had been decorated and garden squares decked out with lanterns which gave a most picturesque effect among the foliage after dark.

Queen Victoria's procession, Edgware Road, 21 June 1897. The vast crowd is finally rewarded with a fleeting glimpse of the Queen as her procession heads towards Buckingham Palace.

Edgware Road by Connaught Place, c. 1905. The offices of J.H. Kenyon, Undertakers and Funeral Carriage Proprietors, occupied this creeper-clad corner before it was rebuilt in 1925 as Connaught Court, one of the smart new apartment blocks which began to transform Edgware Road. At the time of Queen Victoria's Diamond Jubilee, the lavish scale of the decoration on Kenyon's premises excited much comment.

Cambridge Street (Kendal Street) from Connaught Street, *c.* 1904. These long terraces running up to Edgware Road have all gone with postwar redevelopment which included Coniston Court and the twenty-one storied tower, No. 25 Porchester Place. The distant terrace was replaced in 1936 by part of Park West, a vast complex of flats, one of which provided a home from 1947-1948 for famed tenor Richard Tauber.

Porchester Place from Cambridge Street (Kendal Street), *c.* 1905. Another of the many long vanished corners of this part of Paddington with Trotman & Co. the chemists in possession of the single shop. Further along, a pair of bollards guard the entrance to one of Paddington's lost byways, Polygon Mews, while the trees of Norfolk Square are visible in the distance. Smart apartment blocks and new town houses now make up most of this area with the ultra chic Indurrah apartments occupying this corner.

The west side of Portsea Place, *c.* 1905. These were more of the characteristic early nineteenth century houses which were built in the streets off the Edgware Road. The symmetry of the terrace was barely disturbed by the arched entrance to Frederick Mews, centre. These houses still stand and are in a fine state of preservation.

The east side of Portsea Place, *c.* 1905. By contrast, the opposite row of houses, including a more modest home on the right, have all been sacrificed for the building in 1938 of Portsea Hall, another huge apartment complex which included a long frontage to Edgware Road. Part of Cambridge Street (Kendal Street) appears in the distance with a glimpse of the curiously named Rent Day pub which stood adjacent to Sovereign Mews, now all part of Park West.

Crowds in Edgware Road by Grand Junction Road (Sussex Gardens) on the day of King Edward VII's funeral 20 May 1910. King Edward died on 6 May 1910 after a short illness and after a period in which the monarch's body lay in state in Westminster Hall, the King took his last journey through the capital city he loved to Paddington Station from where his body was taken on the Royal Train to Windsor for his interment in St George's Chapel, Windsor Castle. The King, popularly styled 'The Peacemaker', had been a much-loved monarch and Londoners turned out in force to bid him farewell and mark the end of the Edwardian era. Once more the crowds thronged Edgware Road and Grand Junction Road, much as they had done for Victoria's Jubilee and for her funeral some four years later. The buildings of Edgware Road were sombrely draped in purple and violet and a large floral tribute in the shape of a cross was sent to Windsor by 'The Tradesmen of Edgware Road'. The view shows the seemingly inpenetrable crowd in which everyone is wearing a hat despite the hot spring sunshine of the day. A grand carriage procession made its way along Edgware Road and into Grand Junction Road where stands accommodating some 50,000 people had been erected in the gardens separating the main road from the Oxford and Cambridge Terraces. The spectacle of the vast crowds bidding farewell to their beloved King was deeply moving to the numerous foreign monarchs in the procession and the German Emperor was said to have been particularly stirred by the 'striking spectacle'. As may be seen, every window and vantage point was utilised including roof tops, where more intrepid souls clung to the parapets and chimney pots. This panoramic scene includes another piece of Edgware Road before it was transformed by pre-war apartment building – Cambridge Court made an appearance here in 1932. The entrances to Star Street and Praed Street can also be seen, while at the far left an old house marks the future site of the innovative Water Gardens development.

Star Street with St Michael and All Angels, *c.* 1904. The church was an impressive brick built structure dating from the 1860s, running through to Market Street which was renamed St Michael's Street in the 1930s. Damaged by the bombs of the Second World War, the church closed and its congregation was absorbed by St Johns in Hyde Park Crescent, with demolition of St Michael's following in 1967. Star Street and the neighbouring roads of small houses were built in the 1820s for workers from the Grand Junction Canal and when St Michael's School, right, was built in 1870 it included special facilities for the children of the families who worked on the canal.

Edgware Road from Praed Street, *c.* 1906. The terraces on the Paddington side of Edgware Road, right, looked much as they did when the road was first built up but on the Marylebone side, left, they had already been replaced by grander versions. Most were also to be rebuilt on the Paddington side but one still exists, running between St Michael's Street and Star Street even retaining the pawnbroker sign which may be spotted in the picture

Edgware Road from Market Street (St Michael's Street), *c.* 1912. A busy scene which also shows the junctions with Chapel Street and Praed Street, with the clock tower of Gardner's Corner House looking down on streams of early motor buses running on routes whose numbers are still familiar to us. This part of Edgware Road has since been transformed into a mini Manhattan of towering modern blocks, with a large Marks & Spencer store replacing Gardner's on the Marylebone side. The junction with Praed Street stands out with its brightly painted corner block, the present site of the massive Hilton Metropole Hotel.

Praed Street by Edgware Road, *c.* 1905. Local shops included Goy's bicycle store, centre, which also stocked what was then the latest in sound recording technology, Edison Bell wax cylinder records and clockwork driven phonographs to play them on. Messrs Goy also ran a bicycle riding school in an early incarnation of Porchester Hall in Pickering Place (Queensway) – a board seen on the shop also publicises Goy's new roller skating rink at Porchester Hall.

Edgware Road by Praed Street, *c.* 1905. The Midland Bank on the Praed Street corner stands out prominently, while to the right the road narrows as it approaches the Harrow Road junction. The Grand Central restaurant was named after the railway company which had opened its new terminus at Marylebone station in 1899.

The Metropolitan Theatre, c. 1908. The ancestry of Edgware Road's most popular place of entertainment can be traced back to 1524 when the White Lion Inn opened beside the busy road to distant Edgware. A rebuilding in 1836 gave the inn a concert hall and after a further rebuilding in 1863, this became known as Turnham's Grand Concert Hall after its owner, John Turnham. In 1864 the establishment was restyled 'Metropolitan Music Hall' after the newly opened Metropolitan Railway, whose subterranean route passed close by. Yet another rebuilding in 1897 by theatre architect Frank Matcham gave the theatre the appearance seen here. (Maurice Friedman Collection).

The Metropolitan Theatre of Varieties, Edgware Road, c. 1934. The music hall had become a variety theatre by 1925 and by the 1930s the showing of films on Sundays had added to its attractions. In later years there was boxing, wrestling and there were television studios. Until the 'Met's' closure on 6 December 1962 and subsequent demolition, a narrow path ran beside the theatre, its name, White Lion Passage, a link with the original inn from which the old theatre had sprung. Paddington Green police station stands here now.

Newcastle Close, Edgware Road, c. 1960. This byway once formed part of an estate owned by the Crompton and Wild families who built up the land in the 1850s and named the streets after family members and places associated with them. Newcastle Close (originally Mews) came from Newcastle Emlyn, Cardiganshire, from where another family member, Jane Braithwaite, originated. Her name lives on, in Braithwaite Tower on the subsequently rebuilt Hall Estate. Here, the lights shine out brightly on this old Edgware Road corner which still stands amidst the demolition of a future road-widening scheme.

Edgware Road looking south, c. 1912. To the right are the shops on the boundary of the Hall Estate with a taller block where Gilbert Sheldon House now stands. The Church Street corner with the Wheatsheaf pub juts out further along.

The Hall Arms, Church Street by Hall Place, Hall Park, *c.* 1910. The short Paddington section of Church Street runs from Edgware Road to Paddington Green and is thought to date from the foundation of Paddington's first church early in the thirteenth century. In the nineteenth century, shops made up much of the north side of Church Street, and the Hall Arms together with the Lord Collingwood were busy pubs serving the new residential area of Hall Park. Todays scene has been transformed by the postwar rebuilding of the Hall Estate – there is plentiful greenery here now and the twenty-storied Hall Tower overlooks the locality.

Hethpool Street by Cuthbert Street, Hall Park, *c.* 1906. Edwardian gloom pervades a street whose houses, then barely fifty years old, were already overcrowded and run down. The house next to W. Wightman's butchers shop on the Cuthbert Street corner looks rather better cared for.

Hall Place by Cuthbert Street, Hall Park, *c.* 1906. Another view of the old Hall Estate before postwar rebuilding (completed 1973) turned it into a modern complex of high rise towers mixed with low-rise housing. Here, Ferdinand Wieffenbach's bakery on the Cuthbert Street corner provided some visual relief from the drab terraces which were the result of the over intensive building up of the formely rural Hall Estate in the 1850s.

Edgware Road flood, *c.* 1910. The spectacular eruption of a twenty-four inch water main briefly turned Edgware Road into a river and tore up the road's surfacing of tarred wooden paving blocks. Among the victims of the flood was a motor bus whose wheels became trapped in the damaged roadway (see *Images of England Series 'Marylebone'*). The flood occurred between Cuthbert Street and Crompton Street, which is marked here with a large lamp belonging to Henry Ward's Horse Repository where sales of horses were held twice a week.

Edgware Road flood by the Hall Estate, *c.* 1910. A further view of the damaged roadway, which was closed to traffic until repairs could be effected. This took longer than expected, much to the wrath of the Edgware Road traders who issued a postcard highlighting the fact that after 'an eighth of a year' the road had not reopened.

Maida Vale by Blomfield Road, *c.* 1905. The grimy terraces of Edgware Road give way to the elegant mansion flats of its northern continuation, Maida Vale, while to the left, Blomfield Road enters the magical world of Little Venice. Whereas the Grand Junction canal brought industrialization to central Paddington, its extension of 1820 to Camden Town and beyond, the Regent's Canal, created in Maida Vale a landscape unique in London with elegant villas overlooking shimmering waterways. The Regent's Canal passes beneath Maida Vale at this point – Henry Pilgrim's newsagents shop, left, being built over the portal of Maida Hill Tunnel. Prominent in the view are Maida Vale Mansions (1892) which were renamed Cunningham Court in the 1930s.

Maida Vale by Blomfield Road, *c.* 1923. A similar viewpoint with a smartened up Maida Vale Mansions and with fruiterer Walter Wilks in possession of the wonderfully situated shop above the canal tunnel. There is a chic restaurant here now where diners can enjoy unrivalled views of the canal through panoramic windows.

The Regent's Canal with Blomfield Road, left and Maida Hill West, right. Although the canal passed through a well-to-do residential area, it was primarily a commercial waterway as may be seen here as a well-laden lighter makes its way towards Paddington Basin and the Grand Junction Canal. Some of the canal boats were propelled by steam, while others as seen here relied upon horsepower for which towpaths were provided. There is a distant view of the Catholic Apostolic Church, which was designed by J.L. Pearson. It was built from 1891-1893 and was to have had a tower and although work started on it, it was never completed.

Maida Hill West (Maida Avenue) from Warwick Road Bridge, c. 1906. Large stucco fronted villas from the 1840s in a street which is leafier now than in Edwardian days. The term 'Little Venice' for the area around the Paddington waterways is of fairly recent origin, first appearing in the 1930s.

Browning's Pool from Blomfield Road, Little Venice, *c*. 1932. Browning's Pool, formerly known as Broad Water, was overlooked by the Italianate tower of a large mansion which once stood by Harrow Road Bridge, giving a truly Venetian flavour to the scene. The house has sadly gone but from 1954, part of its site was taken for a new public space, Warwick Gardens, now called Rembrandt Gardens. The large house to the right, Beauchamp Lodge, still stands. A pair of canal boats can be seen moored by Browning's Island, the point from which three branches of the waterways diverge.

Regent's Canal from Maida Vale, *c*. 1958. While canals were primarily intended for efficient transportation of freight, they also from the outset accommodated pleasure boats with excursions and a passenger service from Paddington to Uxbridge which was considerably more pleasant than the road journey. The year 1951 saw the first organized pleasure trips on the canal in modern times, when the famous 'Jason's Trip' began to give passengers a unique aspect of London as it journeyed from Little Venice to Camden Town.

Blomfield Road and old Warwick Road (now Avenue) Bridge, *c.* 1905. The Broad Water or Browning's Pool looks tranquil here, but on busy days it would be full of canal boats awaiting access to Paddington Basin. The original brick-built bridge, which carried Warwick Road over the canal, is seen here before it was replaced by a far more urbane structure in 1907. The Browning names hereabouts comes from the poet Robert Browning (1812-1889) who lived for a time in a house in Warwick Crescent overlooking the Broad Water.

Warwick Road (Warwick Avenue) Bridge, *c.* 1912. A steam powered narrow boat glides beneath the newly opened bridge.

Formosa Street, *c.* 1908. Rather than being concentrated in one central High Street, the shops of Maida Vale and Little Venice are scattered about the locality in small groups which give a village-like atmosphere to the neighbourhoods that they serve. Formosa Street, which dates from the mid-nineteenth century, is given distinction by its sharp bend, in the crook of which Maida Hill post office can be seen. The street looks rather dowdy here and the sender of this postcard comments that it is 'not very exciting'.

Formosa Street, *c.* 1920. This is the residential section of Formosa Street leading onwards to the shops, which had been smartened up since the earlier photograph was taken. The classically embellished end wall of the shopping parade is an eye-catching feature, as is the Victorian Prince Alfred pub which is hidden by the tree in the centre of the picture.

Maida Vale, *c.* 1925. Here the character of Maida Vale changes once more with blocks of mansion flats giving way to large Victorian villas set in generous gardens. All of those on the Paddington side, left, have been replaced by the multi-storey housing of the Maida Vale Estate which was built from 1959-1964 by the London County Council.

Clifton Road from Maida Vale, *c.* 1926. Clifton Road is another fine example of a Victorian local shopping street and one which has been rejuvenated in modern times with attractive street furniture and paving. The photograph preserves a busy scene of the 'twenties with blinds protecting the shop displays on the sunny side of the street and a powerful looking steam lorry approaching Maida Vale. To the left is one of the Express Dairy's once familiar tearooms – this one also provided a smoking room.

Maida Vale by Kilburn Park Road, *c.* 1905. Maida Vale ended with this Victorian shopping parade before, in its northern progression, it became Kilburn High Road. In the middle of the row, the local post office shared its premises with a bakery while outside posters advertise the latest attractions at the 'Met'.

Maida Vale Picture Palace, *c.* 1914. This opulent 1,500 seat cinema opened its doors on 27 January 1913 and featured a seven piece orchestra, organ and tearoom. Innovative talking pictures were shown here as early as 1916, proving highly popular as were programmes of pioneering Kinemacolour films. In 1923 the building was renamed the Maida Vale Picture House but it closed in 1940, reopening in 1949 as a club and entertainment venue called the Carlton Rooms. A Mecca Bingo Hall operated here from 1961 and in 1998 the building, by then Grade II listed, became the Islamic Centre.

Three
Harrow Road

Harrow Road by Hermitage Street, c. 1912. While Watling Street (Edgware Road) struck north-westwards from Tyburn crossroads (Marble Arch) in a typically Roman straight line, Harrow Road, which branched off it, was a much more undisciplined affair as it meandered about the countryside through an assortment of Middlesex villages, the first of which was Paddington. Harrow Road bears all the marks of its position alongside London's western transport gateway, crossing the Grand Junction Canal (1801) at several points and skirting the vast Paddington railway complex before, at its London end, becoming absorbed into an array of flyovers and underpasses which brings the great modern highway of Westway into the capital. The new roads drove straight through the heart of old Paddington, removing its town hall and leaving the old parish church of St Mary's an oasis amid the towers of the twentieth century metropolis. Further westward, the Victorians built streets of tightly-packed houses which became overcrowded and rundown before the clearances of the 1960s preceded a new high-rise world of towering flats. The view looks Londonwards with the trees of Paddington Green to the left and the pedimented former Paddington Pariochal School which stood by the long vanished Church Place centre. Of this scene, only Paddington Green survives today beside the thundering highways which have obliterated everything else.

Edgware Road by Harrow Road, *c.* 1930. Harrow Road is seen branching off by the Red Lion pub, left, while opposite a long row of shops curves round the Harrow Road corner. This was the terminus of the electric trams which travelled the Harrow Road as far as Sudbury. The Grand Cinema can be seen on the Marylebone side of Edgware Road, right. The whole scene was transformed when the Marlylebone Flyover was built here in the 1960s.

Building Marylebone Flyover from Edgware Road, 1966. Marylebone Flyover was the first part of the great road scheme which would link the Oxford road, Western Avenue, via the M40 motorway (Westway) to Marylebone Road. The view catches construction work in progress, while in the background the Sovereign Street and Paddington Town Hall area of Harrow Road had yet to be cleared for the building of the motorway itself. The flyover opened on 12 October 1967 but it would not be until 1970 that Westway, London's longest elevated road would open. To the left is the Regal Cinema which opened in 1939 as an Odeon.

St Mary's church, Paddington Green from Harrow Road, *c.* 1905. References to Paddington's first church, a chapel belonging to St Margaret's, Westminster, appear as early as 1222, with a new church dedicated to St James being built in 1678. This lasted just over a century to be replaced by St Mary's (1788-1791), its tiny dimensions a reminder that Paddington was then nothing more than a small village deep in the Middlesex countryside. As London caught up with Paddington and its population increased, a new church dedicated to St James was built in Sussex Gardens in 1845.

Sarah Siddons statue, Paddington Green, *c.* 1906. The statue of Mrs Sarah Siddons (1755-1831), the most renowned actress and tragedienne of her day was unveiled by Sir Henry Irving in 1897. Sarah Siddons lived at Westbourne Farm near Harrow Road from 1805-1817 and her statue portrays her as the Tragic Muse.

Paddington Green by Manor Place, *c*. 1906. Although overwhelmed at times by noise from the motorway, Paddington Green remains a delightfully leafy open space. Relics of the old houses which once bordered it remain, but there are few reminders that this was once the centre of Paddington village. The pleasant corner seen here is now the location of Paddington Technical College dating from 1967.

Manor Place from Paddington Green, *c*. 1912. The residents of these 1880s built red-brick houses would have enjoyed a view of the trees in the disused graveyard of St Mary's church but the street has disappeared without trace and the graveyard is now a leafy open public space. Manor Place was named after Paddington's manor house, which stood close by until 1824.

A dust wharf near Harrow Road, c. 1895. Before the coming of the railways, the canal network allowed freight to be transported to many parts of the country with a speed impossible on the appalling roads but in London the waterways also provided a convenient means for the disposal of vast quantities of household and other refuse. Much of London's garbage was brought to Paddington Basin by road wagons from where it was transferred to barges for shipment to the Thames estuary for disposal at sea.

Harrow Road Bridge, from Browning's Pool, Little Venice, c. 1912. This is one of the points at which Harrow Road crossed the Grand Junction (Grand Union) Canal whose waters narrowed before broadening out into Paddington Basin with its dust wharves, freight transfer depots and warehouses. In its heyday, Paddington Basin handled large amounts of building materials together with hay and manure but its wharves have all gone now and the area awaits rejuvenation as a new waterside quarter of London.

Harrow Road by Sovereign Street with Paddington Green, 1966. Dereliction in Harrow Road with boarded-up properties awaiting clearance for the construction of Westway, which would drive straight through everything shown here. To the right, Paddington Town Hall, which was built in 1853 as Paddington Vestry Hall, awaits its fate, as does old Paddington Green Police Station which is seen in the distance. Sovereign Street, originally called Victoria Street, was one of a group of streets which led to the industrialised North Wharf Road and Paddington Basin.

The Dudley Arms Tavern, Harrow Road by North Wharf Road, c. 1905. This pub dating from 1825 would once have quenched the thirsts of Paddington Basin's canal boatmen. Its rare survival is due to its position on a bend of Harrow Road spared by the all-destroying Westway.

The New Red Lion, Harrow Road by Westbourne Bridge, c. 1905. The splendid leonine figure on the roof surveys the Harrow Road blissfully unaware that the pub would in the 1960s lie squarely in the path of Westway and its switchback underpasses and flyovers. The original Red Lion's history dates back to a more tranquil eighteenth century when this was a delightfully rural spot close to the village of Westbourne Green. However this Edwardian view tells a more urban tale, with the extensive Paddington railway lands in a cutting behind the pub and not a tree to be seen. Behind the camera Blomfield Crescent, which only had seven houses, was one of the tiniest crescents in London.

Bridge Terrace, Harrow Road, c. 1905. Another of Harrow Road's long vanished shopping parades, this one sporting some Bayswater style elegance with its bow-fronts on its run from Fulham Place to Porteous Road. The flats built here in the 1950s were named after Sir John Aird, the first Mayor of Paddington.

Holy Trinity School, Harrow Road, *c.* 1904. Almost every building in Harrow Road to the east of the canal's Lock Bridge has succumbed to motorway building or housing redevelopment, further examples being the Victorian Gothic Holy Trinity School and the adjoining Primitive Methodist Church on the Chichester Place corner right. A further vanished landmark, the Bayswater Jew's Synagogue lay behind these buildings in Chichester Street.

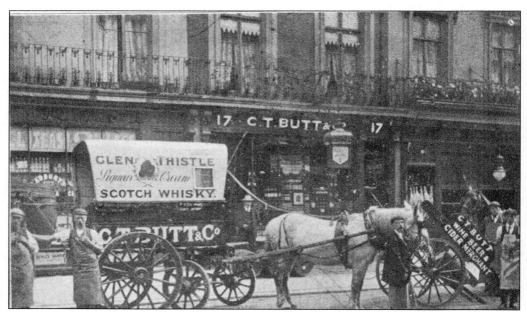

Chichester Street, Harrow Road, *c.* 1904. Chichester Street was a local shopping area with its own post office and an assortment of small businesses including that of wine, beer and cider merchant Charles Butt, who is seen in the doorway of his shop with his staff posed outside. The postwar rebuilding of the entire neighbourhood has removed Chichester Street in its entirety.

Mary Magdalene, Paddington.

St Mary Magdalene, Woodchester Street, c. 1906. Architect G.E. Street cleverly designed St Mary Magdalene to slot into a highly constricted site amid a network of streets which themselves were tightly confined by the curving course of the canal and the Harrow Road. Clarendon Street, right, backed onto the canal and was reputedly the longest street in London without a side turning. The neighbourhood has since been rebuilt but the church which was begun in 1868 and completed ten years later, still towers impressively in its postwar setting of the skyscraping blocks and maturing trees of the new Westbourne Green/Warwick Estate.

Westbourne Square, *c.* 1906. This oddly shaped 'square' only had three sides but its central garden was a welcome touch of greenery in this heavily built up area. Its site is now part of the modern Warwick Estate.

Westbourne Terrace North (now Bourne Terrace) from Harrow Road, *c.* 1906. Densely packed streets to the north of Harrow Road, and to the left the Oliver Arms with its fine lantern on the Oliver Place corner. A succession of side turnings begins with Hasborough Street followed by Stalham Street where sunblinds mark the beginning of a shopping parade. Emily Street is seen further along with Philip Terrace in the distance. The curve of the road is still familiar but the buildings now are all of postwar vintage.

Harrow Road by Westbourne Terrace North (Bourne Terrace) and Torquay Street, c. 1905. This part of Harrow Road was once a shopping centre of some stature serving the populous streets on either side of the main road. The view looks up the hill to the canal's Lock Bridge, beyond which the trees surrounding the Lock Hospital (1842) may be seen. The shopping parade looks attractive here but by the 1960s the shops had fallen into a disgraceful state of delapidation rendering their demolition inevitable. Torquay Street, which still exists, can be seen on the left with the towering Brinklow House dominating the scene today.

Harrow Road from Woodchester Street, c. 1906. It was sale time at E.A. Rudd's, the drapers on the Woodchester Street corner, left, in a view which captures the Edwardian popularity of this shopping area, of which nothing survives today. Both views pre-date the extension of the electric tramway system from Lock Bridge to Edgware Road in 1910.

Waverley Road from Harrow Road, *c. 1906*. Waverley Road was one of the old streets on the south side of Harrow Road where the Brindley Estate now towers skywards. There were costermonger's barrows to compliment the Harrow Road shops and the Ben Jonson Distillery pub, right, to quench the shopper's thirsts. Much of the accommodation in Waverley Road was let out as single rooms resulting in much overcrowding and a squalid environment culminating in a wholesale clearance in the 1960s.

Harry Wright's Champion Outing, Ben Jonson Distillery, Harrow Road, 28 May 1913. Landlord Harry Wright and a good crowd of cloth-capped regulars prepare to set off for a jolly day out to Southend-on-Sea. Pub outings like this were once highly popular and horse-brakes, charabancs or as here, London General buses were hired for the day.

Harrow Road, 1924. A religious procession emerges from Alfred Road and makes its way along Harrow Road passing the Ben Jonson Distillery on the left. The electric tram designated 'Exhibition Car' was heading towards Wembley where the British Empire Exhibition was held in 1924 and 1925.

The last days of the Ben Jonson Distillery, *c.* 1966. The towering new Paddington rises above the battered remnants of the old as the Victorian pub awaits the demolition men. Despite its condition, the building still retains the handsome lines of its upper parts and would probably have been preserved in more enlightened times!

Goldney Road, *c.* 1911. Goldney Road was built around 1860 as part of a new suburb called St Peter's Park on land which was once the property of the Abbey Church of St Peter – Westminster Abbey. The land was acquired for development by members of the Neeld and Goldney families from Wiltshire who named the new streets after their family members and places associated with them. Goldney Road was another local shopping street – the cart is making a delivery to the shop of Alex Strange, wine and beer merchant. A wall poster advertises the Festival of Empire, which was held at Crystal Palace in 1911.

Marylands Road from Harrow Road, *c.* 1911. Another street built by the Neelds with more shops complimented by coster's barrows and the Neeld Arms pub on the Harrow Road corner, left.

Chippenham Road by Goldney Road, *c.* 1911. Chippenham Road makes a straight run from Harrow Road to Shirland Road which is seen in the distance. The tower belongs to St Peter's church (1867), whose eventual replacement by a modern building cost the area one of its more handsome buildings. To the left is part of Chippenham Road's original 1860s housing which would be replaced in 1967 by the dramatic towers of Hermes and Chantry Points. These had a short life, being replaced in 1996 with the low-rise housing of the Walterton and Elgin Community Homes. Chippenham Road is one of the Wiltshire names introduced here by the Neeld and Goldney families.

Chippenham Road by Elgin Avenue, *c.* 1911. St Peter's church is seen again on the right with Sidney Mills' newsagent's shop on the opposite corner left. Chippenham Road was once served by a horse-tram route whose rails can be seen in both views. (see p. 100).

The Prince of Wales Picture Playhouse, Harrow Road, *c.* 1912. The history of cinema in Paddington got off to an ignominious start in May 1909 when Mr Julius Martin of Maida Vale was fined 5s for 'obstructing the highway by exhibiting animated pictures' in Harrow Road. It was, however, much more respectable by 1912 when this purpose built cinema arrived in a blaze of electric light and the promise to 'see the world from an armchair'. When photographed, the cinema was showing the latest 'picture play', *Zigomar versus Nick Carter*, 'the greatest and most thrilling drama ever produced'. Almost as dramatic was the monster stack of timber in the neighbouring Henry Brown builder's yard!

The Prince of Wales Cinema, *c.* 1938. The cinema had been rebuilt in the art deco style of the 1930s and there were 'two super films, a stage show and a band' to ensure a good evening's entertainment. The cinema had succumbed to bingo by 1969 and demolition followed.

The Windsor Castle, Harrow Road, *c.* 1912. A popular Harrow Road pub with a castellated roofline in deference to its name. Beyond is Paddington Guardian's Office (1902) and in the distance, the bright new brickwork of Harrow Road Police Station which had just opened. This section of Harrow Road was once called Windsor Place.

Elgin Avenue from Harrow Road, *c.* 1925. The Elgin names hereabouts originate from the 7th Earl of Elgin who, in 1799 received permission from the Turkish overlords of Greece to remove antiquities from the Parthenon and bring them to England. The antiquities, the Elgin Marbles, were acquired by the British Museum in 1819. Elgin Avenue was a product of the 1860s as the suburb of St Peter's Park took shape and the houses began to spread across the fields towards Maida Vale.

Woodfield Crescent from Elgin Avenue, *c.* 1912. This is one of the lost side streets of St Peter's Park with its houses at the Elgin Avenue end and a row of shops seen in the distance running up to Harrow Road. Frederick Gibb's dairy can be spotted on the Chippenham Mews corner. Woodfield Crescent disappeared with the building of the Elgin Estate tower blocks in 1967.

Great Western Road from Harrow Road, *c.* 1910. In its rural past this was known as the Green Lane but in the 1830s many of the fields which bordered it were acquired by the Great Western Railway for tracks and sidings. The lane was then straightened and renamed after the railway company. The northern section of the road from the canal's Carlton Bridge was called Carlton Terrace until the early 1900s. The police station can be seen, although rather distantly in the centre of the photograph. This would shortly be moved to Harrow Road, the site then becoming devoted to Cinema with the opening of the Grand in 1916 with its later incarnations as the Savoy (1957) and the Essolo (1961).

WESTBOURNE PARK SCHOOLS

Westbourne Park Schools, Great Western Road, *c.* 1907. This large building opened in 1851 on its site beside the Grand Junction Canal at Carlton Bridge but was a further victim of the elevated Westway which dominates the scene here now. Part of the site has also been used for the new Westbourne Park bus garage.

Harrow Road by Bravington Road, *c.* 1920. This view is still recognisable but the London County Council school on the right has gone, as has Harrow Road Market 'the cheapest market in north west London' which was held on the site of the canal's Kensal Wharf. The distant tower belongs to Emmanuel church, which now has a modern replacement.

First Avenue from Harrow Road, Queens Park, *c.* 1908. These modest houses with their faintly Gothic detailing are part of the Queens Park Estate which was laid out on former farm land from 1875 by the Artisans, Labourers and General Dwellings Company. The estate, whose avenues numbered from one to six, is now a conservation area.

Caird Street by Lancefield Street, Queens Park, *c.* 1908. A gathering of local children, one of whom has a hoop, has assembled by James Hutchins' stationery shop which included a post office. The streets on the Queens Park Estate were originally given names consisting of a single letter but due to the unpopularity of this system with the residents, the streets were given 'proper' names. Thus 'C Street' became Caird Street and 'L Street' lengthened to Lothrop Street.

Ilbert Street by Third Avenue, Queens Park, *c.* 1906. The principal shops for the Queen's Park Estate lay along Harrow Road but there were a number of corner shops in the estate's hinterland including Hudson's chemist shop on the Third Avenue corner, dating from 1883. The small tower is a typical architectural flourish on the estate. When first built, Ilbert Street could boast of having London's shortest street name, 'I Street'.

The Avenue Store, No. 109 Third Avenue by Nutbourne Street, *c.* 1908. Mrs Mary Ann Still's grocery shop occupied this prominent position where it was a useful amenity for local residents. The chaotic window display includes still familiar household names including Cherry Blossom polish and Bovril, but 'Veritas Mantles' remind us that most houses were lit by gas in Edwardian times. The building is no longer a shop and is residential in character now.

Queens Park Library, Harrow Road by Fourth Avenue, *c.* 1908. During the course of its first seventy years, Queens Park Library fell under the administration of three local authorities. It opened in 1890 for the residents of Chelsea of which the Queens Park Estate and neighbouring Kensal Town were a detached part. It was then called the Kensal Town Branch of Chelsea Public Libraries, however, in 1901 the southern part of 'Chelsea Detached' was transferred to Kensington and the northern part to the newly created Metropolitan Borough of Paddington, and the library became the responsibility of Paddington who, remarkably, had no other public library of its own until 1924. Upon the creation of the Greater London Council in 1965 and the merger of London boroughs, Marylebone and Paddington became part of the City of Westminster under whose authority Queens Park Library then fell. It is tempting to wonder how many of today's residents on the populous Queens Park Estate realise that their houses were once in Chelsea as few clues are to seen nowadays. The most visible evidence is in Galton Street where an iron street name plate, over a century old, is of a type used by Chelsea Vestry and can still be seen in Chelsea itself in some quantity.

Four
Paddington Transport

In a single century, the nineteenth, Paddington was transformed from a small Middlesex village to a populous Metropolitan Borough, its position in relation to the Cities of London and Westminster with the west and northwest of Great Britain ensuring a future role as a major transport corridor. The story began with the Romans whose straight highways designed to cut journey times crossed the countryside which, in time, would become Paddington. The first canal arrived in 1801 and 1838 saw the opening of Paddington's renowned railway terminus. Paddington then went on to score a number of transport 'firsts' with the opening of London's first street tramway (1861), the world's first underground passenger railway (1863), while as early as 1819 a mechanically propelled road vehicle, a forerunner of the motor car, is reputed to have been demonstrated in Paddington. The arrival of the twentieth century brought increasing mechanization to London's road transport and some of its earliest motor buses were soon travelling the Edgware Road. Numbered bus routes were introduced in 1906 and the photograph catches a London Motor Omnibus Company 'Vanguard' bus at Kensal Rise terminus in that year, when Paddington's famous No. 6 route first appeared. Nearly a century on, the route survives in much of its original form.

De Tivoli's Patent Omnibus, Paddington, 1860. London's first horse bus service was introduced by former carriage builder George Shillibeer in 1829 with a service running from the Yorkshire Stingo pub, just off Edgware Road (on the Marylebone side) to the Bank of England. The innovation proved popular, was joined by others and soon London was criss-crossed by a variety of routes. Levels of passenger comfort were seldom of the highest and conditions inside the horse drawn conveyances were apt to deteriorate, as was observed by one Victorian writer '… the feeling of finding oneself packed into a huge unsightly box or cage-like machine jolting along with eleven other strangers of all sizes and conditions, sitting on each other's coat tails or buried under large volumes of crinoline… .' The writer was referring to the voluminous skirts of the mid-Victorian fashion fad, the crinoline, a particular problem in the cramped confines of a horse bus when an overwhelming surfeit of clothing worn by a lady on an adjacent seat was particularly unpleasant in wet weather. An attempt was made to ease the lot of the bus passenger in 1851 when a bus service in Bayswater gave each passenger a compartment to themselves. The service was unsuccessful but the idea was tried again in 1860 when De Tivoli's Patent Omnibus took to the streets on a service from Paddington's Westbourne Grove to London Bridge via Westbourne Gate, Bayswater, Oxford Street and Holborn. The route usefully connected the railway termini at Paddington and London Bridge and provided six passengers, three on each side of the vehicle, with their own compartment, each one fitted out in the manner of a first class railway compartment with direct access to the conductor via 'Palmer's Patent Signal'. Each compartment had a door which could be closed in wet weather ensuring a degree of privacy previously unknown on public omnibuses. A further compartment at the back of the bus accommodated another four passengers, while those less favoured occupied the exposed seats on the roof. The conductor or 'cad' as he was known, clung to an exposed step at the back of the bus, as is seen in this rare, possibly unique, photograph. Little is known of the eventual fate of this experimental vehicle.

Cooling the horses, Bayswater Road, *c.* 1905. Horse bus designs improved through the later 1800s to the point where twenty-six passengers could be seated in reasonable comfort. It was arduous work for the horses given the state of the roads and the heavy weight of the vehicle they had to draw but there was always a bucket of water and a good feed along the way. This scene was photographed by the drinking fountain which still exists in the Westbourne valley near Kensington Gardens' Marlborough Gate.

A Clarkson steam bus, *c.* 1910. As the old horse buses began to be superceded by their motorised counterparts, a variety of primitive contraptions were tried out on London's population but by 1909 more sophisticated vehicles were arriving including this handsome white-painted Clarkson steam bus which was operated by the National Steam Car Company Ltd. These buses were a familiar sight for a while as they travelled the Bayswater Road on their route from Bank to Shepherd's Bush where this one is seen. They were popular with the public due to the quiet smooth ride they gave.

Kilburn Lane by Salusbury Road, *c.* 1920. A scene on Paddington's northern boundary with a 'B' type bus on route 6 being operated by London General Omnibus Company, the forerunners of London Transport. The 'B' types were London's original standardized buses, the first in a long lineage which culminated in the 1950s with the much-loved Routemasters, some of which are still running. One of the once familiar street fire alarms ('in case of fire, smash glass') is seen on the crowded pavement, left.

Shirland Road, *c.* 1928. The 'B' type buses served London well through the 1910s but following the First World War, further bus development brought the 'K' type into service, an example of which is seen here where it has a peaceful and leafy Shirland Road to itself.

A Bayswater horse bus, *c.* 1905. Another of Paddington's horse buses is seen at its terminus, the Earl Percy pub in Ladbroke Grove. This one's route took it across the width of the borough from Westbourne Grove to Edgware Road, thence onward to Liverpool Street station. This looked a particularly smartly turned out outfit with the driver in a top hat and tartan rug, although the top deck advertisement had seen better days.

Site of London's first tram terminus. Porchester Gate, Bayswater Road, *c.* 1901. An everyday Edwardian scene, but some forty years earlier, excited crowds had gathered to witness the advent of the London tram and maybe take the short ride to Marble Arch. The trams were the brainchild of American George Train who went on to open a similar line in Victoria Street, Westminster. Although the trams worked well, their rails protruded high above the road surface with inevitable disruption as carriages and carts tried to negotiate them. The subsequent public outcry led to the closure of the lines and it would be nearly a decade before trams were tried in London again.

Tram rails in Chippenham Road, *c.* 1908. Trams took to London's streets once more in 1870 but Paddington had to wait until 1888 when the Harrow Road and Paddington Tramway Company began a service of horse drawn cars from Lock Bridge to Harlesden with a branch line along Chippenham Road to link Harrow Road with Carlton Vale. The Harrow Road trams were electrified in 1906 but the Chippenham Road branch had never generated enough business to warrant this modernization, indeed, the service had ended in 1894. However, one horse drawn tram per year continued to run to keep the company's operating powers alive. This was certainly London's most rarely observed transport!

Harrow Road by Fourth Avenue, *c.* 1905. A funeral procession en route for Kensal Green cemetery negotiates the road works accompanying the transition from horse to electric traction for the Harrow Road trams.

Lock Bridge Tram terminus, Harrow Road by Amberley Road, *c.* 1907. The Metropolitan Electric Tramway's service from Harlesden to Stonebridge began on 10 October 1906 and was extended along Harrow Road over the route of the old horse tram service to Lock Bridge on 22 December 1906. The photograph dates from the earliest days of the new service with some local youth joining the crew for their traditional picture.

Harrow Road by Elgin Avenue, *c.* 1907. A 'C' type electric tram travels the Harrow Road bound for Lock Bridge passing as it does so the premises of tailor Isaac Alexander, a latter day 'Alexander the Great' if his shop front is to be believed. The tram is seen in its original condition before covered tops became the vogue and the upper deck was enclosed.

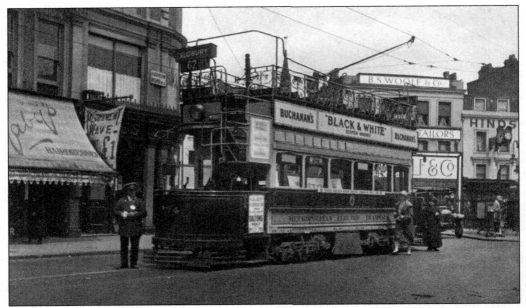

Paddington Tram terminus, from Harrow Road by Edgware Road, c. 1930. The tram system was extended to Edgware Road on 6 December 1910 allowing passengers to connect with the new Bakerloo Tube and the multitude of Edgware Road bus routes.

A trolley bus at Paddington Green, Harrow Road, c. 1960. Harrow Road's electric trams lasted a mere thirty years before being replaced in 1936 by trolley buses which also took their power from overhead wires. The terminus at Edgware Road had to be abandoned as there was insufficient room to turn the trolley buses round (the trams could be driven from either end). A new terminus was created at Paddington Green where a turning circle ran round the green. The trolley buses had an even shorter life than the trams and were replaced by buses from 1962. Paddington's old town hall is on the left.

Near Edgware Road station, *c.* 1905. London and the world's first underground passenger railway, the Metropolitan, opened on 10 January 1863 with a line from Farringdon Street to Paddington (Bishops's Road). The novel form of transport proved popular with Paddington's residents who for the first time were able to travel to the City without the constant battle through the congested streets. Other lines, including the District Railway and the Inner Circle became established and used Edgware Road station, which is seen here at a time when the old steam trains were being replaced by new electric ones.

Royal Oak station, *c.* 1903. Railway services from Hammersmith to the City began on 13 June 1864 with Royal Oak station opening on 30 October 1871 to serve the residents of the newly urbanised Westbourne Green area. Great Western Railway trains also used the station which is seen sporting some fancy rooftop ironwork before it was rebuilt in red brick. The girders of a rebuilt Lord Hill's Bridge now partly obscure the station.

The Central London Railway, *c*. 1901. Electric trains arrived in Paddington for the first time on 30 July 1900 when the Central London Railway, with its twopenny flat fare, introduced a deep-level tube service from Shepherd Bush to Bank. This was the beginning of the Underground's Central Line and provided local stations at Queen's Road (Queensway) and Lancaster Gate. In the line's earliest days, the carriages were drawn by electric locomotives as seen here. The wooden platforms would not be allowed today due to fire risk.

Queen's Road (Queensway) station, *c*. 1903. The Central stations were built with variations on the style shown here, one of the largest being Queen's Road. The stations were designed to be built on, but spent their first years as single storey structures – Queen's Road was shortly to be topped by the Coburg Court Hotel, see p. 24. The richly toned terracotta of the station has sadly been obscured by modern paint.

Lancaster Gate station, *c.* 1920. Lancaster Gate was one of the smaller Central stations and is another which spent its early life as a single storey building before being topped by the Park Gate Hotel in red brick and matching terracotta. The station's surface buildings were replaced in the mid-1960s when the towering Royal Lancaster Hotel was built on the site, with road widening setting back the building line by some distance.

Elgin Avenue with Maida Vale station, *c.* 1922. Paddington's second deep level Tube was an extension of the Baker Street and Waterloo Railway, the Bakerloo Line. The first section of the railway opened on 10 March 1906. Extensions were added on 27 March 1906, first to Marylebone (then called 'Great Central'); to Edgware Road on 15 June 1907; to Paddington on 1 December 1907, and then to Kilburn Park on 31 January 1915. Maida Vale station which is noted for its fine tile work, opened on 6 June 1915 with an entirely female staff due to the numbers of men fighting on the continent during the First World War. The station has changed little externally in nearly ninety years.

A Tube train carriage in transit, Elgin Avenue. The sight of a Tube train carriage progressing along the street is not one that the residents of Elgin Avenue may expect to often see. This example, having completed the first stage of its journey from the manufacturers by rail, then took the overland route through the streets of London to the Tube depot. The heavy haulage by old fashioned steam power was undertaken by a company whose name is still familiar, Messrs Pickford the removers.

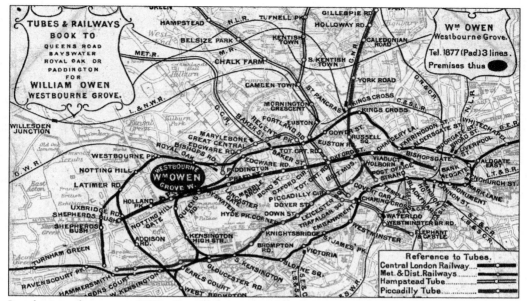

London's railways, *c.* 1909. A useful map produced as a postcard by Westbourne Grove department stores William Owen (see p. 42), doubtless as an aid to help clients find the store. The Bakerloo Tube had only reached as far as Paddington station in 1909.

Paddington Station, *c.* 1850. Paddington's name will forever be linked with its renowned station, the Great Western Railway's London terminus which opened on what was then the perimeter of the city on 4 June 1838. It all looked rather ramshackle in 1850 - Eastbourne Terrace in the background looked more impressive – but greatness was close at hand and the mighty smoke-wreathed cathedral arches of Isambard Kingdom Brunel's grand design were going to impress the Victorian train traveller from the opening day of a new Paddington, 29 May 1854. The new terminus lay slightly to the south of the old one.

Paddington Station, *c.* 1930. One of Paddington's original trio of train halls with its 700ft long glass vaulted roof spans and one of the pair of transepts which cross them.

King George VI's funeral train, Paddington 15 February 1952. The sudden and unexpected death of George VI on 6 February 1952 shocked the nation, the popularity of the late King ensuring that on the day of his funeral there would be vast crowds lining the streets to bid him farewell. The funeral route was the traditional one with the cortege entering Paddington at Marble Arch and passing through the solemn mass of onlookers in Edgware Road before reaching Paddington station. From there, the funeral train bore the late King away from the capital for interment at Windsor.

The Great Western Hotel, Praed Street by Eastbourne Terrace, c. 1920. Main line railway termini usually have a grand hotel in close proximity, the one at Paddington was built for the Great Western Railway from 1851-1854. It was designed by P.C. Hardwick on a grander scale than had previously been seen for a railway hotel, with 115 bedrooms and numerous sitting rooms. The Praed Street façade featured an impressive pediment with typical Victorian sculptures of Peace, Plenty, Industry and Science, the work of designer John Thomas. Much of the hotel's external decoration was removed when the hotel was remodelled in the 1930s.

Eastbourne Terrace, c. 1922. The platforms of Paddington station are below street level with ramps leading down to them, one of which is seen on the right. The tall town houses of Eastbourne Terrace (whose name is the antithesis of the local Westbournes) were in use as small hotels catering for the railway trade. All were replaced from 1958-1962 by a dreary row of office blocks.

A sightseeing car, Paddington Station, c. 1908. In addition to its railway services, the Great Western Railway operated a number of sightseeing cars in which visitors to London were taken on a tour of its major attractions. The steeply raked rows of charabanc-style seats and large windows on this Milnes-Daimler motor ensured that everyone had a good view. The car shares the cobbled ramp from Praed Street onto the station concourse with a hansom cab and a horse bus while a youthful sailor looks on. (J.M. Cummings collection).

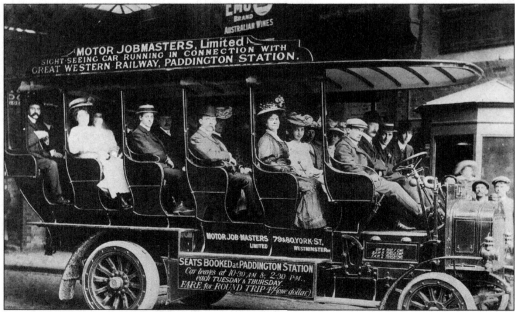

A sightseeing car, Paddington station, c. 1907. A well-laden car demonstrating the popularity of these tours. This one was operated by Motor Jobmasters Ltd of Westminster who, with an eye on the American market, priced the tour at one dollar or four shillings, at a time when there were five dollars to the pound. (J.M. Cummings collection).

Five
A Paddington Miscellany

Praed Street by London Street, c. 1903. Praed Street runs from Eastbourne Terrace to Edgware Road and was named after William Praed, the first chairman of the Grand Junction Canal Company, the Paddington stretch of which opened in 1801. The canal company acquired many acres of land surrounding the canal's terminal at Paddington Basin and development of the area soon followed with the Edgware Road end of Praed Street completed by 1828, as were the more modest side streets like Star Street and Sale Place whose houses were built for canal workers. The western end of Praed Street came later and was slightly grander in scale. Praed Street rapidly developed into a shopping centre to serve the burgeoning local population, while proximity to Paddington station attracted much railway related business. A typical example was the Great Western Trunk Stores on the London Street corner, right, with part of its stock of luggage piled up outside the shop. The Load of Hay pub, left, was also well placed to catch the thirsty traveller as he emerged from the station.

Praed Street, August 1902. An amateur photographer's snapshot captures the scene as a carriage procession and mounted escort emerges from Paddington station at the time of Edward VII's coronation. The King had travelled to Victoria station from Cowes following the illness which had delayed the coronation originally planned for June 1902 but other members of the Royal family had travelled to Paddington from Windsor.

The Great Western Hosiery Co., Praed Street, c. 1914. Another business to adopt the name of the local railway company was the Great Western Hosiery Co. who traded from several addresses in Praed Street. The well-filled shop windows reveal a fine range of gentleman's clothing including cloth caps at 6s 6d, straw boaters at 7s 6d and an alluring display of Aertex gentleman's 'combinations'.

Praed Street, *c.* 1905. A further range of shops in Praed Street, part of the long terrace running from London Street to Cambridge Place (now Norfolk Place).

Praed Street, *c.* 1908. The plain brick terraces beyond Cambridge Place (Norfolk Place), right, date from Praed Street's earliest days, the 1820s, when the canal company began to build on its land. The long row of small shops culminated in the Grand Junction Arms which was named after the canal company. The terrace has gone now but similar buildings can still be seen to the south of Praed Street. Part of St Mary's Hospital is on the left.

St Mary's Hospital, Praed Street, *c.* 1904. As Paddington's population grew in the early nineteenth century, the need for a new hospital resulted in the building of St Mary's, the foundation stone of which was laid by Prince Albert on 28 June 1845. The hospital in Cambridge Place (Norfolk Place) opened in June 1851 and in 1854 a medical teaching facility was provided. Further expansion continued and 1904 saw the opening of the hospital's Clarence Wing, which is seen here as the last of the builder's hoardings were about to be taken down. St Mary's renowned Lindo Wing was opened in 1937 and was the birthplace of Prince William (1982) and Prince Henry (1984). A Professor of Bacteriology, Alexander Fleming, famously discovered penicillin while working at St Mary's in 1928.

St Mary's Hospital, *c.* 1920. A comparison view to that above showing few changes in the intervening years, with very modest properties adjoining St Mary's Hospital including the Somerset Arms pub and Youatt's Hotel which are visible in both views.

114

Street accident, Eastbourne Terrace by Paddington station, *c.* 1921. The facilities of St Mary's Hospital were close at hand for the victims of this hair-raising incident which left a motor lorry hanging precariously above the ramp leading into Paddington Station. The background of Eastbourne Terrace shows the Paddington Sailors and Soldiers Club. (J.M. Cummings collection).

At Buckingham Palace, *c.* 1913. Few businesses can aspire to a job at Buckingham Palace but when the palace's familiar Sir Aston Webb designed façade was created in 1913, Paddington's William Boyer & Sons, sand, gravel and ballast merchants, were on hand to supply washed pit-sand to the project. The company, whose premises were at Irongate Wharf, Paddington Basin, delivered the sand to the palace in this magnificent steam lorry and in such circumstances a photograph is *de rigueur*, although the palace was all but obscured by the vast constructions fronting the building works.

Warwick Avenue, *c.* 1920. Warwick Avenue can claim to be one of the widest residential streets in London, its grand Victorian panorama originally culminating in the landmark of St Saviour's church and its tower of Kentish ragstone. The church by Thomas Little was built from 1855 but by 1972 its stonework had become unstable and the church was demolished with a new St Saviour's and an apartment block taking its place in 1976. The slim modernist spire of the new church attempts to recreate the focal point of its predecessor. The view shows one of the pair of entrances to the Bakerloo line's Warwick Avenue station which opened on 31 January 1915, one of a small number of early Tube stations to have no surface buildings. The width of Warwick Avenue is such that the wooden cabmen's shelter, right, a relic from the days of the hansom cab, is actually in the middle of the road.

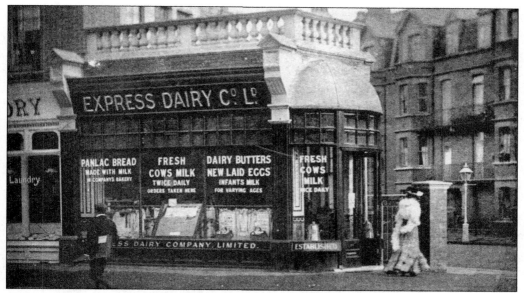

Express Dairy, Lauderdale Parade, Elgin Avenue, *c.* 1908. Lauderdale Parade is another of Paddington's local shopping terraces, its appearance little changed from Edwardian days although there are, of course, different businesses here now. The photograph was taken to celebrate the opening of a new branch of the Express Dairy Company in premises that are now occupied by a flower shop.

Hughesdon & Hinds, Estate Agents, 22 Lauderdale Mansions, *c.* 1911. By the 1890s there were few undeveloped sites remaining in Paddington, the last of them being in the Maida Vale area. The remaining fields were built on during the Edwardian era with grand blocks of red brick mansion flats lining leafy new streets. The firm of Hughesdon & Hinds had a variety of flats on offer in seven of the local mansion blocks where two to four bedroomed apartments were available at rents from £40 to £110 per annum with amenities including liveried porters.

Elgin Avenue by Morshead Road, c. 1908. The lofty gabled mansion blocks of Elgin Mansions run away towards the horizon while to the right, Biddulph Mansions climaxes with a pair of domes by Lauderdale Road. The lowlier building by Morshead Road, left, was of an earlier vintage – it has since been replaced by a modern mansion block whose design echoes that of its neighbours.

Sutherland Avenue by Castellain Road, c. 1908. These houses were built in a more traditional London style in late Victorian times and appear little changed since the time of this photograph. Castellain Road, left, reveals the distinctive street naming style introduced by the Metropolitan Borough of Paddington, the names being made up of white ceramic letters fixed onto a dark painted background.

Elgin Avenue by Portsdown Road (Randolph Avenue), *c.* 1905. The first part of Elgin Avenue, then called Elgin Road, was begun in the 1840s from the Maida Vale end and was a spaciously laid out boulevard which could easily accommodate the meagre traffic of the day. The Edwardian scene looks equally peaceful and an elegant street lamp could survive in the middle of the road without the protection of bollards.

Elgin Avenue by Portsdown Road (Randolph Avenue), *c.* 1905. Multi-coloured Victorian brickwork, arched windows, and between the shops, candy-twist columns distinguish this shopping parade which ends with the Lord Elgin Hotel on the Elgin Terrace (now Lanark Road) corner. The nearer corner was occupied by the bakers, Lowe & Sons who were established in 1861.

Portsdown Road, (Randolph Avenue) from Elgin Avenue, *c.* 1911. The street is dignified by the group of houses on the left which date from 1862 and feature a wealth of unusual architectural detail and polychromic brick work. Part of the end house of Elgin Mews South with its Gothic window is seen on the left.

Wymering Mansions, Wymering Road, *c.* 1905. A lively slice of Edwardian street life with a hansom cab, baker's boy with his baskets, a youthful newspaper seller, a dairy cart ('pure country milk') and further along the street, a household remover's wagon in evidence as a tenant moves into one of Wymering Mansion's recently completed flats. The street itself was created around 1901.

Essendine Road, *c.* 1906. An army of broom wielding street cleaners descend upon Essendine Road, with what is presumably their foreman standing centre-stage in the middle of the road. The street was a product of the 1890s, its surfacing of rolled dirt and stones requiring constant attention to keep it in good order and a water cart to lay the dust in dry weather.

Essendine Road School from Shirland Road, *c.* 1908. This facility was provided by the School Board of London and is seen here when quite new. The spindly saplings, which can just be seen, have since grown to maturity to soften the urban image.

Coronation Fete. Paddington Recreation Ground

Paddington Children's Coronation Fete, 27 June 1911. By 1886, a large area of north eastern Paddington remained in a semi-rural state with areas of allotment gardens, however, gradually the streets and mansion flats of the new Maida Vale began to cover the last of the open land. A precious twenty-seven acres were saved from the builders and the amenity of Paddington Recreation Ground with its notable sporting facilities was laid out, the first section of it opening in April 1888. From its earliest days when Jubilee celebrations were held in it, 'Paddington Rec' has held a special place in the hearts of the local residents. Following the success of a children's coronation fête held at the time of the coronation of Edward VII and Queen Alexander in 1902, a similar event was staged for the coronation of George V and Queen Mary in 1911. The King and Queen had been crowned in Westminster Abbey on 22 June 1911 and five days later, 13,000 of Paddington's younger elements were treated to a splendid party in honour of Their Majesties. The children from Paddington's schools were assembled at three points around the borough; Kilburn Lane School, the Town Hall and St Michael's, Star Street and with a lively band at its head, each group processed to the recreation ground for the festivities. It was a beautiful midsummers day and once all the youngsters were in place they were given an entertainment lasting one and a half hours. The photograph shows a troupe of acrobats entertaining the children who were all clad in their Sunday best, the white dresses and fancy hats of the girls standing out well in the picture. The display included community singing of patriotic songs and a verse of the National Athem, while one of the most popular parts of the day was a display of Brock's daylight fireworks. As one observer put it '… it was a pretty sight to see the joyous juveniles waving their little flags'. There was also an address by the Mayor of Paddington. Having fun is a thirsty business, however and at teatime, the souvenir Coronation beakers which had been distributed earlier were filled with a much needed drink of ginger beer.

Shirland Road by Braden Street, *c.* 1908. Shirland Street was laid out in the 1860s with the houses arriving during the 1870s, the line of the road following the course of the now unseen Westbourne stream. To the left, the Shirland Hotel, now the Truscott Arms, guards the entrance to Elnathan Mews while Braden Street to the right, once a street of small houses is now merely an access way to a modern estate of flats. (Tony Davis collection).

Maida Vale Skating Palace and Club, 1910. February 1910 saw the opening of this, the largest roller skating rink in the world with a width of 110ft and a length of 500ft. From the outset the rink became a fashionable resort for devotees of a pastime which had been popular from Victorian days, while others could enjoy the resident band, the restaurant or just promenade around the perimeter. The fad for 'rinking' soon declined and the premises closed in 1912 taking on a more mundane role as National Insurance offices. Entertainment returned in 1934 however, when the BBC created its Maida Vale Studios here.

Delaware Road, *c.* 1909. Delaware Road was laid out around 1907 on the last open land to the south of Paddington Recreation Ground. With it came Delaware Mansions continuing the tradition of mansion flat building hereabouts. The flats overlooked an empty site opposite which was just about to be developed as the Maida Vale Skating Palace.

Delaware Road, *c.* 1912. A similar viewpoint with the skating rink in evidence, although this was already in a forlorn state, its brief fashionable life gone and a drab role as National Insurance offices imminent. It would be another two decades before music and entertainment would return to this remarkable building.

St Augustine's School, Kilburn Park Road by Rudolph Road, *c.* 1906. St Augustine's School and the great landmark church also dedicated to St Augustine stand opposite each other, both dating from 1871 (see p. 2), but while the church endures, the school is now housed in modern premises. To the left of the trees is a pair of houses where the Kilburn Sisters, a group of Anglican nuns, established their Orphanage of Mercy in 1875.

Kilburn Park Road from Shirland Road, *c.* 1908. This was the boundary between the boroughs of Paddington and Willesden (Westminster and Brent since 1965), with a long terrace on the Paddington side right, which still stands. The Willesden side is to the left but here everything has gone and monolithic concrete tower blocks dominate the scene. The great steeple of St Augustine's church is still a commanding presence on the skyline.

Carlton Vale, *c.* 1905. Carlton Vale, originally Carlton Road, dates from the 1850s and accommodates a popular local pub, the Carlton Tavern. The original Carlton Tavern is seen here before perishing during a Zeppelin raid in 1918 during the First World War. The modern flats of Keith House now adjoin the pub in place of the terrace seen here.

Canterbury Road from near Queen's Park station, *c.* 1905. Another section of the Paddington/Willesden boundary and one which is barely recognisable today. On the Willesden side left, the houses of Denmark Road have been replaced by an estate of flats, while to the right, Paddington's territory has seen a transformation into the low-rise flats of Western Court, Carlton Vale.

The Quadrant, Kilburn Lane, *c.* 1906. The Paddington/Willesden boundary extended from Maida Vale to Harrow Road with the northern and western extremities of the Queen's Park Estate running along it. More of the estate's small but distinctive houses are seen on the left by Ilbert Street together with Edward Field's grocery shop.

Mozart Street from Bravington Road, *c.* 1908. Mozart Street gave its name to a large housing estate, which from 1971 began to replace the houses in the far distance. The street itself was a creation of the mid-1880s and was partly given over to local shops, one of which was the splendidly named Mozart Farm Dairy, centre.

Fernhead Road by Shirland Road, *c.* 1911. A lively scene in Fernhead Road as local children gather outside Henry Duffill's stationery, tobacco and confectionery shop with its eye-catching window displays of picture postcards. It was more sedate next door at St Peter's Park Wine and Spirit Stores which was run by Mrs Sarah Pattenden – the handcart at the kerbside had presumably just topped up her stock of Brandon's Rustic Ale. Arthur Sargeant's bakery was to the right with Charles Reeves' greengrocery all but obscured by its sunblind, left, in a shopping parade, which survives to this day.

Acknowledgments

The selection of historic photographs in this book has been enriched by the contributions of Maurice Friedman and Tony Davies while transport historians R.W. Kidner, David Brewster and J.M. Cummings have contributed rare photographs and sound advice. The input of all of them is gratefully acknowledged, as are the wonderful facilities of the City of Westminster Archives Centre; Camden Local Studies and Archives Centre; and Guildhall Library. Books consulted include; *The London Encyclopaedia*, Ben Wienreib and Christopher Hibbert; *London Street Names*, Gillian Bebbington; *The Buildings of England, London North West*, Nikolaus Pevsner and Bridget Cherry; *Guide to Bayswater*, John Wittich and James Dowsing; *Little Venice*, James Dowsing; *Marylebone and Paddington*, Richard Bowden; *Dial 'M' for Maida Vale*, Kevin O'Sullivan; *Edgware and Willesden Tramways*, Robert J. Harley; *Westbourne Grove*, Gloucester Court Reminiscence Group; *Victoria County History* Vol IX; *The Lost Boys*, Andrew Birkin.

Printed in Great Britain
by Amazon

12990896R00075